SONGS AND POEMS OF A COMMON MAN

A Plain Man's Words in Poems and Songs

Rev. Gordon Langford

SONGS AND POEMS OF A COMMON MAN

Copyright © 2014 by Rev. Gordon Langford

All rights reserved. No part of this book may be reproduced or transmitted in any form or by any means without written permission of the author.

Printed in the United States

ISBN-13: 978-0-9904764-0-5

ISBN-10: 0-9904764-0-5

Ezekiel Press
PO BOX 5172
Kingwood, Texas 77325

For information concerning the contents of this book:
Please write to Rev. Gordon Langford
1309 So. Holly Ave.
Cleveland, Texas 77327
Or email:srmlangford@yahoo.com

About Myself

My name is William Gordon Langford. I was born in a frame farm house in a community called Turkey Creek, just outside Plant City, Florida, and just east of Tampa, Florida, on June 26, 1928. I was born at home, not in a hospital or clinic. My parents were farmers. My father's name was Lennie Gorde n Langford and my mother's name was Jewel Emma (Musselwhite) Langford. My father passed away in 1970, at the age of 72. My mother passed away in 1981. She was 76 years old. I had a brother born before me, but I never knew him. He died of whooping cough at the age of six months. I am the oldest of the living children. I had a brother who was five years younger than me. His name was Ralph Donald Langford. He passed away in 2010. His home was in Fernandina Beach, Florida. His wife, Betty Jo, still lives there. Betty Jo is a wonderful Christian lady. I love her like she was my real sister. I never had a real sister, but she is like one to me. I have another brother who is 15 years younger than me. His name is Harvey Jerrel Langford. He lives in Tampa, Florida. He is divorced and lives alone but under the careful watch care of his only child, a super fine young lady named Laura Lynn Goncalves, who also resides in Tampa, Florida.

I attended Hillsborough High School in Tampa, and at the age of 17, I talked my father into signing for me to join the U.S. Navy. It was at the end of World War II but still during the duration of the war. I spent two years in the regular Navy and seven and a half years in the Naval Reserves. While in the Navy, I did some deep sea diving. After being honorably discharged from the Navy, I went back to school. Then later I married a pretty little Texas girl named Lorraine Ruth Jackson. She was four days short of being 16 years old when we got married at her parents' home in Orange, Texas. I was 20 years old. We had three children. First was a daughter. We named her Ruth Ellen Langford.

She now lives in Orange, Texas. Then we had a son. We named him Timothy Wayne Langford. He now lives in Powell, Wyoming. Then we had another son, whom we named Stephen Ray Langford. He lives in Cleveland, Texas. Steve is a bachelor, Tim is a divorced bachelor, and Ellen is a widow. Ellen and Tim each have two sons. Ellen's sons are Tony and Troy. Tim's two sons are Joshua and Jacob. My beloved wife of 45 years (actually four months shy of 45 years) went to be with the Lord on June 19, 1993. After she passed away, I thought for a while I would lose my mind. Lorraine and I got married in 1948, and about a year later I got into an apprentice cabinet maker's program on the GI Bill and learned the trade of cabinet maker, and for 52 years I was a commercial cabinet maker.

Of course, during that time, I did other things too. In December of 1949, my young wife and I accepted Jesus Christ as our personal Savior and Lord. We were baptized in January, 1950. At that time, we were living in Lutz, Florida, just north of Tampa. In 1954, we moved to Orange, Texas, and I got a job in a cabinet shop in Port Arthur, Texas. We joined the Little Cypress Baptist Church and soon began working with the youth in Training Union and Sunday School. Lorraine was also active in the Women's Missionary Union (WMU). On May 28, 1961, I answered God's call to the ministry. Soon after-ward, my Pastor had me preaching on the radio at least once a month, and also I was being sent to other churches real often to fill in for Pastors who were sick or away for some reason. I preached in many churches in southeast Texas and southwest Louisiana. I preached my first radio message on August 13, 1961. My first time preaching away from home was at North Liberty Baptist Church in Sulphur Springs, Texas, on August 27, 1961. My first time to preach as a pastoral supply was at Jones Prairie Baptist Church in Leggett, Texas, on September 3, 1961. I performed baptismal services for the first time at Little Cypress Baptist Church on September 8, 1963. My first pastorate was a new mission we named

Bancroft Baptist Mission, located in Orange, Texas, sponsored by Hartburg Baptist Church near Dew-eyville, Texas. I was at that mission 14 months. During that time, I attended seminary extension classes at Magnolia Avenue Baptist Church in Beaumont, Texas. I studied Old Testament Theology, New Testament Theology, and Hebrew History. On May 1, 1966, I was called to be Pastor of Trinity Baptist Church in Beaumont. On May 6, 1966, I was ordained at Hartburg Baptist Church. I conducted my first communion (Lord's Supper) June 26, 1966. My first funeral service was May 27, 1967. I was at Trinity for five years. I was working at a secular job all that time, and I changed jobs and went to work in Houston, Texas, and resigned my pastorate at that time. My family and I moved to Tarkington Prairie, near Cleveland, Texas, in March, 1972. We soon joined Rural Shade Baptist Church where we worked in Sunday School and various other positions until I was called to pastor Friendship Baptist Church in Kenefick, Texas. I was there about 16 months, but my job kept sending me all over the U.S., installing store fixtures, and I resigned the pastorate there. In 1997, I met my present wife, Lynn Marie Colson. Actually, I already knew her but not very well. She and Lorraine were room mothers together at the school where our children attended. Lynn's oldest son, John, and our youngest son, Steve, were best friends. They are the same age. Lynn has three children, same as I do. Her children are also a daughter, Theresa, a son, John, and a son, David. I'm very proud to call them my stepchildren. Lynn and I were married October 24, 1997. We now live in Cleveland, Texas. I worked in Beaumont for a total of 32 years, plus a year and a half in Houston building and installing bank and store fixtures plus other types of businesses such as hospi-tals, clinics, law offices, libraries, air terminals, etc. I was retired when Lynn and I got married. I worked part-time for a while, but in the year 2000, I had triple bypass heart surgery. It slowed me down.

Lynn is a wonderful God-loving woman. We support each other in our service for the Lord.

When I was 14 years old, I learned to play a few chords on the guitar. A family friend taught me the basics of playing by ear. I played at some church functions and birthday parties but never got deep into my playing. In 1978, I had an industrial accident that left my left hand mangled and my wrist stiff. I could not play my guitar at all, so I sold it and did not bother with music anymore for 18 years, although, at times I did miss my guitar. When Lynn and I got married in 1997, her mother had a Fender guitar which had belonged to her deceased husband. She told me to take it and play it. I started fooling with it and began to work out my own system and find my own way to hold the chords until I finally could play along with friends. With those friends and my wife encouraging me, I soon began participating in the singings that many of the local churches have on weekend nights. Lynn and I joined Harmony Church in Shepherd Texas, and I soon was asked to be associate pastor. We were there about three and a half years, and while we were there, the church began having a singing once a month, and they still do. I may be a bit biased, but I think Lynn is a good singer. She likes to sing and, of course, the only kind of music we know is gospel music. I now play with a country gospel band called Glory Bound Express. We are an amateur band that plays at nursing homes on a regular schedule and sometimes at special occasions. Lynn still works at this time, but we still get to several of the singings each month. Lynn and I have a ministry of our own called Sold Rock Ministries of Cleveland, Texas. Our main ministry is the publication of a monthly bulletin we call "Gospel Singing Time". This ministry has been blessed so much. The bulletin has a monthly schedule of the area singings plus a brief message and other items. I still preach about once a month at our church. We belong to Faith,

Hope, and Love Church in Livingston, Texas. I write songs and poems sometimes when inspiration strikes me. That's what this book is about.

I have been married twice, and both times God has given me a godly, Christian wife. God has been so good to me. There were times when I would find myself off track, and yet God was there convicting me and directing me back to where I needed to be. God has been by my side in some pretty serious situations. In the year 2000, I had that open heart surgery, which the doctors said saved my life because the blood vessels in my heart were so blocked I would be dead in two weeks or less. Yet I have never had a heart attack. In 2008, I had carotid artery surgery in my neck. The doctor said we got to it just before I would have had a stroke. Yet I have never had a stroke. In 2013, I had abdominal surgery. The doctor said it was a good thing I went to the hospital when I did because I could have died before the day was over. Yet God was with me. At this writing, I am 85 years old. I ache and hurt in places I never knew I had, and my joints are getting stiff and my stamina is not what it once was, and yet I still drive where I want to go and I play my music in nursing homes where many of the residents are younger than me. I still do some chores at home, and I still enjoy life. God is GOOD. I thank Him every day for my family and friends, who are some of the world's greatest people. I will put a title to my name here because my dear wife asked me to, but, normally, I am not big on titles. Hope you get some enjoyment from this book.

Rev. Gordon Langford

Acknowledgments

This book would not have been possible without the help of family and friends. I deeply appreciate my friend Dale Bianchi's contribution to getting this book published. He has taken care of most the things that many people are not aware of that goes into a project like this. Also I cannot thank Betty Masters enough for her time and work in proof reading and correcting my mistakes in my original material.

There are others who have helped with the financing of this book and with the support I needed. I can only say thank you and I love all of you more than you know.

A special thanks also goes to Rev. David Yanez, my publisher for making this book financially possible. Most of all, I thank God for using these people to get the job done and for His great inspiration in most of the material in this book.

To my wife, Lynn, thank you honey for encouraging me along.

Rev. Gordon Langford

Foreword

There are many men that I wished I would have had an opportunity to meet in my lifetime, one of them being Fred Rogers of Mr. Rogers Neighborhood, What a great man he was!
I met Gordon Langford in the spring of 2010 at a flea market where I own a small shop selling guitars and sundry items. He had stopped in to have a look and take a rest from walking around the market. When he picked up a guitar I noticed his mangled left hand, which I later learned had been run through a table saw with a dado blade in it. He had only half a forefinger and the rest were set in a way that allowed him to chord the guitar a little easier. I thought to myself, "What an inspiration this old guy is, still playing guitar after such a tragic injury." What I didn't know at the time was that he didn't play his guitar for years after the accident.
From that point on, Brother Gordon has been a regular in my shop, every Saturday and sometimes Sunday too! My shop has moved two times and has grown into a very successful business: Highway 59 Music, Guitar Parlor and Scrub Shop. . I owe Brother Gordon a big heartfelt thanks for helping grow my business by just being there. He still comes in every Saturday and we attend singings together regularly! I consider him a friend much like the friendship between David and Johnathan in the bible. We have a Covenant relationship and I couldn't ask for a better friend than Gordon Langford. I can honestly say," Now that I know you, I am so glad that I met you"

Dale Bianche
Highway 59 Music
Guitar Parlo & Scrub Shop

Table of Contents-Poems

A Beautiful Place 17
A Christian Always 18
A Highway Trip 19
A Little Girl's Song 20
A Prisoner's Thought 21
An Act Of Terror 22
Biblical Characters 23
Birth Of Jesus 24
Christmas 25
Christmas Season 26
Christmas Time 27
Church 28
Cold 29
Courtship 30
Dad 31
Death 32
Decisions 33
Evening Shadows 34
Faith 35
Fear 36
Forest Scene 37
Full Moon 38
God And Me 39

Golden Years 40
Greed 41
He's Coming 42
Helping Others 43
I Want To See Him 44
Idle Moments 45
In Love Again 46
Jesus Is Coming 47
L Bar J 48
LeAnn 49
Let Us Sing 50
Life's Highway 51
Lonely 52
Lorraine 53
Love Is 54
Lynn 55
Married 56
Mom 57
Money 58
My Beloved Wife 59
My Lord Is Real 60
My Old Car 61
My Woman 62
Mystery Of Nature 63
Nancy 64
Nature's Peace 65

No Show 66
Now She's Mine 67
Observations 68
Our Wedding 69
People Watching 70
Pondering 71
Pray 72
Remembering 73
Sarah 74
Satan 75
Saved 76
Sneeze 77
Someday 79
Something To Think About 80
Spontaneously 81
Summer Morn 82
Sunday Morning 83
Sunday School 84
Thank You, Lord 85
The Auction 86
The Barber Shop 87
The Bible 88
The Bird 89
The Bridal Show 90
The Cattle Shed Event 91
The Country Road 92

The Dark Red Rose	93
The Devil	94
The Difference	95
The First Easter	96
The Forest Fire	97
The Men's Restroom	98
The Mermaid	99
The Mountain	100
The New School	101
The New Year	102
The Passing Of Time	103
The Pawn Shop	104
The Small Cabinet Shop	105
The Small Town Cafe	106
Time	107
To Build A Church	108
To Start The Day	109
Today	110
Tracy	111
Troubled World	112
War	113
Wendi	114
When We Were Wed	115
Winter Storm	116
Work	117
You Outshine Them All	119

A Beautiful Place

The evening sun was setting beyond the still smooth sea,
Bringing a feeling of peace and contentment to me.
I walked along the beach's white sand,
And thanked God for giving us this great land.
There are wars and troubles around the world today,
Making me want to just go away;
To the ocean's edge and a sandy beach,
All life's troubles are left out of reach.

A Christian Always

I went to church last Sunday,
Had a great time with the Lord.
Then came Monday;
I had to lean on God's Word.
The devil, he chased me all week long,
Always tempting me to do something wrong.
But I don't belong to Satan;
I'm not his to claim.
The Christian I am on Sunday,
On Monday I am the same.
I do no false pretenses;
I never put on a show.
No matter what day God should call me,
I'm always ready to go.

A Highway Trip

A long highway, a consumer of time,
Between Houston, Texas, and North Caroline.
Many big trucks and cars of all kinds,
Some old and ugly, others new and fine.
Speed limits vary from place to place,
But for the most part, it's like a hot rod race.
Every now and then there is an accident;
People get hurt and vehicles get bent.
We must drive safely, handle our cars with care,
To reach our destination if we want to get there.

A Little Girl's Song

I saw a beautiful little girl,
With eyes pretty and bright;
And a sweet happy smile,
That showed gleams of heaven's light.
She was standing in church,
Singing what Jesus meant to her;
The congregation was very quiet,
I didn't see a person stir.
A radiant glow was on her face,
Her voice was a sweet melody;
She sang of Jesus' "Amazing Grace",
Her words stirred my soul within me.
I made a decision to turn from the world,
As God's spirit moved me within;
And I believed in the words of that little girl,
I trusted Jesus and turned from my sin.
The words of that great old song,
She sang so lively and bold;
Changed my life and turned me around,
And saved my sinful soul.

A Prisoner's Thought

It's such a struggle just to live,
No one seems to care;
Yet we have so much to give,
And like with others, we'd like to share.
Sometimes we feel,
So sorry for ourselves;
We think we are at the bottom,
And there's no one there to help.
"What can I do?"
I ask, from this prison cell;
I would take on any task,
To be free from this manmade hell.
This old earthly flesh and bone,
A prison cell can hold;
But with all its steel and stone,
It cannot contain my soul.
Though I'm in a prison cell,
And not out running free;
I can know I'm doing well,
For God is always here with me.
When I'm feeling helpless and bound,
Things are not as they should be;
I will not let Satan get me down,
Or get the best of me.

This poem was written for a friend's son.

An Act Of Terror

The sky was clear,
Beautiful and blue;
Some small white clouds,
But only a few.
A very light breeze,
Was faintly blowing;
But for what lay ahead,
There was nobody knowing.
The plane climbed high,
In a lazy way;
Just a routine flight,
On a normal day.
Then suddenly there came,
A loud blasting sound;
And bits and pieces,
Were falling to the ground.
Flesh and metal,
All in shreds;
Not a person left alive,
All were dead.
Someone had planted,
A bomb on board;
Down in the hold,
Where the luggage was stored.
An act of terror,
No one knows why;
So many innocent people,
Had to suddenly die.

Biblical Characters

Moses was the greatest leader,
Of all the Israel race;
David defeated the giant,
Man to man, face to face.
Daniel slept with the lions,
Paul studied in a prison cell;
Jonah was swallowed by a whale,
A story we all like to tell.
Samson was a tower of strength,
And feared by those round about;
Peter cut off the soldier's ear,
And Thomas was the one to doubt.
John lived alone in exile,
Lazarus was raised from the dead;
Samuel walked with God as a child,
John the Baptist lost his head.

Birth Of Jesus

In the Bible, many stories are told,
Of places, events, and men so bold;
I like to read all about them,
The best one happened in Bethlehem.
This is where Mary and Joseph went,
And stopped at the Inn when day was spent;
No room at the Inn they were told,
The Innkeeper sent them back out in the cold.
Mary was laboring, about to give birth,
To the most precious child born on the earth;
They finally stopped at a cattle shed,
Where the child was born, a manger for his bed.
The surroundings were lowly for this newborn King,
But the shepherds nearby heard the angels sing;
They arose from their night watch and said with a shout,
"Let us go see the One the Angel told us about."
Later the wise men came from far away,
Traveling mile after mile day after day;
They presented their gifts of things they had,
They worshipped the Child while they felt so glad.
This story that I'm telling here,
Is why we celebrate Christmas each year;
This Child was Jesus, our Savior and King,
And like the shepherds, I can hear the angels sing.

Christmas

The tree was decorated with tinsel and lights,
And many ornaments to make it look right;
Presents were spread all under the tree,
Some for my wife; some for me.
The wrappings were bright in red and green,
What I liked best was the manger scene;
Telling the story of Jesus and His miraculous birth,
How He came from heaven to visit this earth.
He was loved and welcomed, hated, and scorned,
But the most precious child that ever was born.

Christmas Season

Christmas time once more is here,
It's a happy time of goodwill and cheer;
We celebrate the season every December,
It's a time for us to reflect and remember.
As we wrap our gifts once by one,
Make the top of your list God's precious Son;
We are celebrating the Christ child's birth,
He left the glory of heaven and came to earth.
He came with a purpose and a mission to do,
In a few short years, He would die for me and you;
He came to give us a new way of life,
And deliver us all from our sins and strife.
Though He died so cruelly there on the cross,
His death was a victory, surely not a loss;
He was resurrected; He came out of the grave,
To rule as Lord over all who are saved.
So at this time of year with so much to do,
Take time to remember that Jesus loves you.

Christmas Time

Christmastime is here,
Time for peace, love, and cheer;
Shopping for that special gift,
Many are feeling a spiritual lift.
Decorations are hung on the tree,
Gifts are wrapped for you and me;
Money is rapidly being spent,
Later we may wonder where it went.
There is a Santa in every store,
Enticing people to come buy more;
I wonder if people really know,
As on with the celebrations they go.
That Jesus Christ is the one who,
We all should be looking to;
It matters not if we have gifts or trees,
What is in our heart is what God sees.
So let us celebrate the birth of God's Son,
And wish a Merry Christmas to everyone.

Church

There is a place where I like to go,
Where I can feel relaxed around people I know;
I can join them in song and praising the Lord,
I can hear a message preached from God's Holy Word.
This place is known to me as a church,
Where I can go when my heart hurts.

Cold

The cold is sharp,
It cuts like a knife;
Winter brings to me,
A miserable life.
I never can seem,
To get warm enough;
Thought I dress in thermals,
Jackets and stuff.
The cold cuts deep,
Like a love gone wrong;
When you've lost your true love,
And you feel all alone.
The cold causes me,
To shake and shiver;
My eyes feel glazed,
Like ice on the river.
I can hardly wait,
For spring to get here;
And let me know,
That summer is near.

Courtship

The thrill of a courtship, the excitement and fun,
Of a love that's worked for and a love that's won;
Though a marriage may be the ultimate goal,
The road to get there is good for the soul.
Music and movies and eating out,
Are all worth the trouble and thinking about;
You can go sightseeing or maybe to the beach,
The love you're seeking is not out of reach.
Buy your lady gifts and take her places,
Perhaps to a rodeo or maybe to the races;
No matter where you go, you're not taking a chance,
Soon you will find that thing called romance.
Take your time, go a little slow,
And if you really love her let her know;
When the goal you feel is now in sight,
And everything seems to be just right.
There's one thing left for you to do,
Whisper to her these words, "I love you."
She will welcome you in her open arms,
And share with you all her wonderful charms.
Though her love you may have won,
Your lifelong courtship has just begun;
Court her daily the rest of your life,
And she will always be your loving wife.

Dad

In June comes Father's Day,
Don't let it slip by and get away;
Take a tip from me, here's what to do,
Give him a hug and say, "I love you!"
When I was just a mere little lad,
I always wanted to be with Dad;
Dad worked hard from morning 'till night,
Yet he always took time to teach us right.
Dad's days were spent in back-breaking toil,
Trying to make a living from that black Florida soil;
On Sunday, all in the family would know,
Get up, get dressed, and to church we would go.
Those days are all past, Dad is now gone,
All of those memories are now mine alone;
If it's possible, tell your dad how much you care,
And on this day pay honor to fathers everywhere.

I wrote this poem on a Father's Day, in memory of my Father.

Death

The curtains were drawn; the blinds were closed,
A chill came over me from my head to my toes;
In that room death was there,
I could feel its presence permeating the air.
But I knew this was not my day,
So I told Death to go away;
It's not my time; I can feel it in my bones,
So just go on, Death, and leave me alone.
I know it is appointed unto men once to die,
Although I cannot fully understand the reason why;
I feel deep down within me,
This is not my time appointed to be.
I opened my eyes; I moved my hands,
I tried to get off the bed; I wanted to stand;
I was on my feet standing on the floor,
I started to walk slowly towards the door.
It was a miracle of God that saved me that day,
From the cold hand of death as I walked away.

Decisions

Today there are many things to do,
New things to start, old things I didn't yet get through;
Early now, I must make a choice,
Will my decision be bad or will it make me rejoice?
Decisions, decision on every hand,
All I can think of is to do the best I can;
I give to God my adoration,
As He speaks to me and gives me inspiration.
He is here in my darkest hour,
And gives me strength through His great power;
He is there when I laugh or smile,
He loves me tenderly and walks with me every mile.

Evening Shadows

The evening shadows lay across the road,
The sun was sinking like a heavy load;
The shadows are reminding of the day that is past,
The end of a day's work, going home at last.
The sun is still there but sinking rather low,
The shadows are getting longer, stretching ever so slow;
But I will soon be home and sit down to rest,
It's the time of day that I like best.

Faith

It's something we cannot see,
But we can know when it's there;
It's something we always need,
When we go to God in prayer.
Though it may not be seen,
It's something we can feel;
Like a warm sunbeam,
We know it's very real.
We can look back,
And see where it's been;
We can look ahead and know,
That it will be with us then.
It picks us up when we feel low,
We must have it to realize our dreams;
We can never ever have too much,
We never have enough it seems.
As we walk with God and feel His touch,
It's a thing called "Faith", I've heard;
And it can even move mountains too.
I have read about it in God's Word,
His way of speaking to me and you.

Fear

Fear can sometimes be good,
But often times fear is bad;
Often it is not understood,
And causes us to feel real sad.
It can cause us to shake,
Or it can cause us to run;
It may keep us awake,
Or spoil all of life's fun.
I sometimes feel this awful fear,
And feel that trouble is somewhere near;
But troubles come and troubles go,
Leaving me with this thought I know;
That no matter what life brings,
Things rarely are as bad as they seem.

Forest Scene

The forest is dense; the foliage is green,
Wildlife all around me, though rarely seen;
I smell the blooms on the Magnolia tree,
And listen as nature speaks to me.
The birds enjoy their freedom; here and there they fly,
I hear the rustling of the brush as a rabbit hops by;
A squirrel dances on an oak tree limb,
Unaware that I am watching him.

Full Moon

The night is light,
The moon is bright,
Its face beams down on the world.
By happen chance,
I may find romance,
And fall in love with a beautiful girl.
I think I will go,
Where the dancing is slow,
And the music plays soft and sweet.
While I am there,
If I look with care,
I may find the girl I would like to meet.
Shine on, shine on, Mister Moon,
Maybe you can lead me soon,
To the fulfillment of my fantasy.
And through it all,
I may fall,
For a girl who cares for me.

God And Me

The morning sun is shining bright,
Chasing away the darkness of the night;
The birds are singing their melody,
While my thoughts are centered on God and me.
His artwork is seen in the morning sky,
His presence grows stronger as the day goes by;
When problems come and troubles I face,
I know He is there with His loving grace.

Golden Years

The golden years,
I hear them say;
Is when our eyes grow dim,
And our hair turns gray.
When our teeth fall out,
And wrinkles appear;
It seems we have reached,
Our golden years.
Most of our time,
Is in memory;
Of all the things,
That used to be.
We look at tomorrow,
And we wonder what's in it;
Living our time each day,
Minute by minute.
We may be in laughter,
Or we may be in tears;
But still we are enjoying,
Those "Golden Years".

Greed

Torment and restlessness,
Found on every hand;
The stars are laughing,
As they look down on man.
He has gone over the edge,
His insanity knows no end;
He will cheat his neighbors,
And he will lie to his friends.
If there is a chance,
Of monetary gain;
He doesn't care,
About the suffering and pain;
That he brings to others,
As he travels his way;
And fills his pockets,
While others pay.

He's Coming

I look off into the sky,
And sometimes I wonder when Jesus is coming again;
But I'm really not worried as long as I am living my life for Him.
Jesus is coming! Oh Yes! He's coming again,
To gather all His children from this world of sin;
This world is a mess, getting worse with passing time,
In the Bible it tells us that it is all a sign.
We better start living God's own way,
He's coming again just any day!

Helping Others

If in my abundance others I should help,
Have I gained in heaven any merits for myself?
What is my help for others really worth,
If done without sacrifice here on earth?
A soldier's duties are expected of him,
It's his place in the service to obey all of them.
No medals are given for being a soldier good and true,
Who only does what he is expected to do.
Medals are given to those who sacrifice,
And go beyond their duty at the risk of their life.
The Bible tells us to go the extra mile,
When a brother is down, give him more than a smile.
Give him your coat if he's cold and you know,
And by sacrificing you may give him your cloak also.
If you find yourself down and know not what to do,
And you see a neighbor in distress who needs help too;
Do you say, "Sorry, my friend; I'm also down,
And being pushed further it seems into the ground?"
Or do you start looking, trying to find a way,
To be of help to your neighbor today?
The Bible teaches us to put others first,
And we will be rewarded in heaven for what we do on earth.

I Want To See Him

I want to see the mountains with their snow-capped peaks,
I want to see the valleys with their winding creeks;
I want to see a cornfield with stalks growing high,
I want to see a rainbow circling through the sky.
I want to see a jungle with its nature there so wild,
I want to see the happiness of a beautiful little child;
I want to see the seashells lying on the sandy beach,
I want to see the horizon, but it's always out of reach.

Idle Moments

Sitting in the park on a bright sunny day,
Looking at a field lark while little children play;
The bird runs lightly over the ground,
The children yell and jump up and down.
Some play ball; some are on a swing,
The bird ignores it all; I can hear him sing;
The grass is green; the air is warm,
The children are happy; they are doing no harm.
The bird is free, looking for food,
The things I see put me in a good mood;
If the whole world could be like this,
It would be a place of real happiness.

In Love Again

I once had a romance with a lady named Melissa,
But we parted through circumstance, and I really don't miss her;
For into my life suddenly there came,
My future wife, Lynn is her name.
She is a lady so very fine,
She's pretty and nice, and now she's mine;
She is warm and cuddly, like a soft teddy bear,
And when I come home, she is always there.
I like to watch her as she moves about,
Makes me want to hug her and say with a shout;
"I love you, I love you! Lynn, my sweet dear,
I want to have and hold you through the evening years."

Jesus Is Coming

Get ready! Get ready!
Is the warning cry;
Jesus is coming again,
The time draweth nigh.
The world is in chaos,
It seems to be insane;
So many without God,
Living their life in vain.
The rich get richer,
It seems their only goal;
Even if it costs them,
The death of their soul.
The poor are struggling,
But they seem to stay down;
No matter what they do,
They can't make any ground.
For those without Jesus,
Their hope is all gone;
The saved go to meet Jesus,
The lost are left here alone.

L Bar J

The room is full; the noise is loud,
The old, the young, make up the crowd;
Jokes are told and lies are swapped,
Feet are scuffling on a floor just mopped.
Laughter is heard throughout the place,
Hardly a frown is seen on any face;
The waitresses are busy running every which way,
It's a weekday morning at the L Bar J.
In Cleveland, Texas, on Houston Street,
Sits this little café where the people meet;
The stories are many; the tales are tall,
As the deer antlers hanging there on the wall.

LeAnn

I know a lady whose name is LeAnn,
She's a good friend to this old man;
I can talk to her about things on my mind,
She listens to me as I talk every time.
She tells me about things in her life,
The good and the bad, the happiness and strife;
She is as pretty as a lady can be,
Her face lights up when she smiles at me.
LeAnn, I wish you all the happiness life can give,
And wish only the best for you as long as you live.

Let Us Sing

Let us sing songs of joy,
Let us sing songs of praise;
Let us make our music,
In all the many ways.
We can sing about God's love,
And about His Amazing Grace;
We can sing about heaven,
That wonderful, glorious place.
There are songs about Jesus,
And when He shall come again;
And the meeting in the air,
When He gathers all His children in.

Life's Highway

While traveling along on life's highway,
For every wrong turn, we soon have to pay;
There are hills to climb and valleys below,
Where we meet many problems, as we all know.
So keep on track with your eyes on the road,
Don't get over-burdened with too heavy a load;
We can allow ourselves to get in a bind,
With too many problems that trouble our mind.
Be careful how you take the curve,
Look for the bumps in time to swerve.

Lonely

Loneliness is a state of mind,
There is a remedy I hope to find;
To lift me out of gloom and despair,
Can happiness be found anywhere?
Though I stand among a crowd,
Voices and laughter are very loud;
I can still feel so all alone,
As if I was a long way from home.
I must try to shake off the gloom,
And join the crowd in the room;
There is no special reason to feel this way,
I guess it's just one of those days.
Sometimes I just feel so low,
With nothing to do and nowhere to go;
I need not worry, I'll be okay,
Just a matter of letting God have His way.

Lorraine

For forty-five years you were my wife,
My reason for living, the center of my life;
I loved you truly, my dear Lorraine,
But now my life is filled with sorrow and pain.
You always stood with me; you were there by my side,
From before we were married until the day you died;
There are many fond memories that you left behind,
Though they have passed, they still cross my mind.
Our three children and grandchildren too,
Are the surest reminders I have of you;
Now I know that you are there,
Resting in the arms of God's loving care.

Love Is

Love is a walk through the mall,
Love is when we sit and talk;
Love is when we laugh and joke,
Love is doing the things we like most.
Love is sharing a dark red rose,
Love is playing with your toes;
Love is when I rub your feet,
Love is seeing your smile so sweet.

Lynn

Did you ever know a lady called Lynn?
That's the name of my new girlfriend.
Her hair is black and rather short,
Her eyes are brown and real, real dark;
I like to be with her as much as I can,
She seems to be happy that I am her man.

Married

The people quieted down,
The music started to play;
Then I turned around,
Feeling so nervous on this day.
There she was, the one I love,
Slowly walking through the door;
A sight I had been thinking of,
Since I entered a short while before.
Her dress was beautiful and long,
Her face was brightly glowing;
The musicians played our song,
Her happiness was showing.
The minister spoke of matrimony,
I wished that he would hurry;
And end this wedding ceremony,
But there was no need to worry.
It was soon over and done,
As we left there together;
My wife and I both have won,
For our love will last forever.

Mom

Today is very special for mothers everywhere,
It's when we take the time to show them how much we care;
I can remember my own mother, the things she did and said,
It leaves in me an empty spot, for Mom has long been dead.
When I was young and went to school, every morning Mom would say,
"Son, do you have a hanky in your pocket? You may need it today."
Life wasn't so easy way back then,
We never seemed to have much money to spend;
Mom and Dad worked hard there on that old farm,
Every evening they would be so tired with aching feet and arms.
When I was ten, I wanted to learn to play the guitar,
But we didn't have much money, we didn't even have a car;
From the Sears catalog Mom ordered my first guitar,
Three dollars plus shipping; back then money went far.
There are so many things that come to my memory,
That my mother did for my brothers and me;
She loved us dearly and spent her life,
Doing her very bet to bring us up right.
So I thank God for my mom and mothers everywhere,
Who teach their children right and tell them about God's love and care.

Money

Money is something we all seem to need,
But with some people, it only fosters their greed;
Some people are so downright greedy,
They wouldn't give a bread crumb to the needy.
For many people, money is good,
It helps us accomplish the things we should;
But money isn't always so easy to get,
We labor and toil, we work and we sweat.
"We have it made!" we may sometimes say,
Then something happens to take it all away.

My Beloved Wife

Forty-five years of my life,
I was married to my beloved wife;
I loved her dearly through those years,
We laughed together and shed some tears.
Our life was just simple and plain,
Not much money, but no need to complain;
Our three children were the results of a love,
Put together and bonded by God above.
Now she's gone; God called her away,
To a better place and a happier day;
I know that over on eternity's shore,
She is resting with God forevermore.

My Lord Is Real

The Lord is my shepherd, (Psalm 23:1)
The Lord is my sight; (Luke 7:21)
The Lord is my protector, (Psalm 23:4)
Yes, the Lord is my might. (Psalm 29:1)

The Lord is my harp, (I Samuel 16:16)
The Lord is my string; (Psalm 33:2)
The Lord is my music, (2 Chronicles 7:6)
The Lord is my king. (Psalm 29:10)

The Lord is my staff, (Psalm 23:4)
The Lord is my rod; (Psalm 23:4)
The Lord is my strength, (Psalm 28:7)
Yes, the Lord is my God. (Psalm 30:2)

The Lord is my help, (Psalm 28:7)
The Lord is my shield; (Psalm 28:7)
The Lord is my Savior, (John 3:16)
Yes, my Lord is real. (Complete Bible)

My Old Car

I had an old car,
It would seldom run;
But when it did,
I had plenty fun.
It would shake and rattle,
Squeak and groan;
But give it the gas,
And it would move on.
The seats were worn,
The tires were bare;
Fenders were bent,
And rust everywhere.
The radio worked,
And the horn would blow;
But the brakes were bad,
And oil pressure low.
But that old car,
Was all mine;
It was paid for,
I didn't owe a dime.

My Woman

Her legs were long,
Her hair was blond;
Her blue eyes sparkled,
Like a magic wand.
Her teeth were white,
Her skin was smooth;
She moved so graceful,
With every move.
Her lips were like honey,
They were very sweet;
She had all the right curves,
From her head to her feet.
She looked like a doll,
And acted like a queen;
She was the prettiest woman,
I have ever seen.
Then one day it all,
Came to an end;
Not another day on earth,
Would this beauty spend.
Now I am so lonely,
My heart is in distress;
How I wish once more,
I could feel her caress.

Mystery Of Nature

The rain falls; the grass grows high,
The hot sun shines; the grass will die;
Nature has mysterious ways,
It gives moonlit nights and cloud-darkened days.
Often times storms arise,
Tornadoes swoop down from the skies;
Earthquakes cause the earth to quiver,
Winter cold makes one shiver.
Springtime lets the flowers bloom,
You know hot weather will be here soon.

Nancy

Her beauty was a thing to behold,
As she walked about with grace;
She held her head erect and bold,
But carried a smile on her face.
Her stature was small and petite,
Her blond hair was done real well;
Her clothes were so trim and neat,
She was very confident, I could tell.
She looked and she smiled at me,
There was something I wanted to say;
She was the loveliest girl I ever did see,
And my words seemed to just melt away.
I heard my voice give a low utter,
She smiled again and said "Hello";
Then I heard myself begin to mutter,
As I said, "Your name I want to know."
"Well," she said, "My name is Nancy,
And though I may look well to do;
I am not really all that fancy,
And I think I would like to be friends with you."
That is how it all began,
The changes that came into my life;
She has made me feel like a man,
It is really great to have her for my wife.

Nature's Peace

Standing on the side of a hill,
Overshadowing a brook with its waters still;
There stands a tall tree taking a sunbath,
While near its base is a winding path.
The path leads along through the peaceful wood,
Past a few rotten old boards where a cabin once stood;
Out here there is no shove or push,
Buds are sprouting on every bush.
It's a place of solitude and peace,
Where a troubled life can come and find release.

No Show

Multicolored lights flooded the stage,
A loud noise was heard from a crowd in rage;
A star was scheduled to give them a show,
But where he was no one seemed to know.
The tickets were all sold, the people all there,
But the entertainer seemed to be elsewhere;
Do the stars really care for their fans,
Who helped them achieve their lifelong plans?
I know there are some who don't seem to care,
But then there are others who are always there.

Now She's Mine

I went fishing and caught a wife,
Now she's mine for the rest of my life;
I threw out the bait; she grabbed it unawares,
Of my wily ways or my tricky snares.
I took my time and gave her some line,
Then I reeled her in, and now she's mine;
I was not fishing to catch a fish,
I was carrying out my long-time wish;
To catch this woman to keep her for all time,
My luck was good, and now she's mine.
I love you truly, my dear Lynn,
I'm so glad I reeled you in.

Observations

The morning stillness overwhelmed me,
With the early sun all about me;
I watched a little squirrel race up a tree,
And sit on a limb as he looked down on me.
I saw a young rabbit who was in no rush,
As he hopped from beneath a small leafy bush;
A bird was descending from the sky above,
Bringing to my mind God's wonderful love.

Our Wedding

The way you walked into my life,
I knew someday you would be my wife.
Some things I know are just meant to be,
The look I saw in your eyes;
I couldn't help but realize,
That you are the one meant for me.
I know that in God's master plan,
There is a woman for every man.
And for me that woman is you,
Now I give to you my love;
The kind that comes from heaven above,
This is my promise to always be true.
When God smiled on me that day,
I could tell right away,
That my life would never be the same.
As we go through life together,
We can face all kinds of weather,
Because at last I give to you my name.

People Watching

I watched the people walking down the street,
Some not my type, others I would like to meet;
I saw an old man in a bright gaudy shirt,
Walking with an old lady in a short mini skirt.
I remember the young girl dressed like a slouch,
Her boyfriend with earrings, carrying a pouch;
There was a drugstore cowboy with a 10-gallon hat,
I sure hope I never look like that.
A woman was wearing her high-heeled boots,
Some men were dressed in business suits;
I saw some with their head in the air,
While others just didn't seem to care.
Some were in a hurry, some going slow,
Some knew where they were, others didn't know;
One went by walking with a swagger,
Then there was one who could only stagger.
Long hair, short hair, and in between,
Some of the weirdest things I have ever seen;
Then it was time for me to scoot,
Wearing my spotted shorts and cowboy boots.
My ear-bob caught in my long, stringy hair,
I can't understand why the people stare.

Pondering

I was sitting and thinking late one night,
Relaxed and resting in the low lamplight;
Things came to my mind that I would ponder,
About life in general that caused me to wonder.
I wonder about technology and how everything works,
I wonder about nature with all of its quirks;
Then there are people, so many different kinds,
These thoughts overwhelm me and nearly blow my mind.
Then comes this one sobering thought,
Someday all these things will come to naught.

Pray

The greatest need in this world today,
Is kneeling Christians on our knees to pray;
Talking with God, discussing our troubles and woes,
Keeping in touch with heaven wherever we might go.
In school, at work, at home, or at play,
We should never neglect an opportunity to pray;
Praying is an honor which God has bestowed upon us,
It is much better to talk with God than with each other, to fight and fuss.

Remembering

One day I decided to go for a hike,
Off through the forest where it is peaceful and quiet;
I walked along on a well-worn trail,
My eye caught a glimpse of a bushy squirrel's tail.
I came to a spot that seemed so serene,
A few flowers were blooming and the grass was green;
I sat down on a fallen tree,
And began to reflect on things that used to be.
I thought back to when I was a boy,
The friends I had and my favorite toy;
I remembered when I first drove a car,
And how I learned to play the guitar.
But now I'm older; my hair has turned gray,
Yet I still enjoy living each and every day.

Sarah

A small little girl, just nine years old,
With a pretty smile and personality so bold;
With long brown hair and eyes so bright,
When things are gloomy, she is a shining light.
To know her is a blessing gained,
Who is she?
Sarah Smith is her name.

Satan

Satan is busy running about,
Destroying people's lives within and without;
I try real hard to avoid his snares,
I know in my heart God really cares.
But sometimes Satan's deceit is so strong,
He tempts and leads me to do things wrong.

Saved

The world was in sin; the devil thought he had won,
But then God sent His begotten Son;
He came with a purpose and a mission to do,
He would die on a cross for me and for you.
God said heaven was not made for sin,
Anyone guilty would never enter therein;
But when Jesus was crucified,
"Father, forgive them!" were the words He cried.
And all who believe and trust in Him,
Will not have to bear the guilt of their sin.

Sneeze

I once had a sweetheart,
Her name was Louise;
But the smell of her perfume,
Always made me sneeze.

We walked along the beach,
Enjoying the ocean breeze;
But the fresh salty air,
Made me want to sneeze.

We walked in the forest,
Among the brush and trees;
But the pollen in the air,
Made me want to sneeze.

We went walking through the snow,
We were about to freeze;
When a snowflake tickled my nose,
So, you know I had to sneeze.

We went to the library,
The sign said, "Quiet Please";
But when a book fell from a shelf,
The dust made me sneeze.

We were sitting in the theatre,
I gave my girl a squeeze;
A whiff of her hairspray,

Sneeze

Caused me to sneeze.

We went to a café,
She ordered ham and cheese;
And just as she took a bite,
You're right, she had to sneeze.

Someday

Someday Jesus is coming!
I know it won't be long;
We should all be rejoicing,
And praising Him in our song.
Someday the trumpet will sound,
I long to hear Gabriel's note;
We read about it in God's Word,
We will experience the things He wrote.
Someday Jesus will send the angels,
To gather every Saint;
It will be a glorious picture,
No artist could ever paint.
Someday Jesus is coming!
He has already paid the cost;
To erase all our sins,
Though most people are still lost.
Someday it will all be over,
The gates of hell will open wide;
The lost will be screaming,
Searching for a place to hide.
Someday judgment will be made,
On those who turned Him down;
Their weeping, wailing, and gnashing teeth,
Will be a terrible sound.

Something To Think About

I was walking along the street one day,
When I saw a small boy who seemed busy at play;
He looked up at me with a tear-dampened eye,
And said, "Mister, do you think I'm too big to cry?
My daddy's a drunkard and Mommy's never home,
Sister ran away, and my big brother's gone;
My big brother loves me; he calls me his little man,
But he's in the Army, serving Uncle Sam.
I often feel lonely and want to run away and hide,
Mister, do you really think that I'm too big to cry?"

Spontaneously

Spontaneously we sang without practice or forethought,
"Sing us a song," the people said, so suddenly we were caught;
We sang a song I had written several months in the past,
I always like it because the tempo is a little fast.
Seems I sometimes forget a line here and there,
But the people always listen and seem not to care;
Lynn always reminds me of the lines I forget,
So if we sing enough spontaneously, we will someday get it yet.

Summer Morn

Sitting by the window on this early summer morn,
Basking in the sunlight and already getting warm;
Thinking and wondering what this day will bring,
Whether joy and happiness or sadness and pain.
Every morning holds secrets of things yet unseen,
As the dew on the grass gives luster to the green;
Watching the sunrise with its sharp, harsh glare,
Reminding me always of God's loving care.

Sunday Morning

It's Sunday morning; church bells are ringing,
It seems I can hear the people there singing;
There's a peaceful stillness in the air,
I can see and feel it everywhere.
The sun is shining brightly; the sky is clear,
It is very obvious that God is near.

Sunday School

In Sunday School we try to teach,
The Word of God to those we reach.
We learn more about the great love of God,
And the paths on earth that Jesus trod.
The trials that Jesus had to go through,
To save the sinful souls of me and you.
If you think you may already know,
Everything to help you spiritually grow;
Just go to Sunday School, you will soon find out,
What Christianity is all about.

Thank You, Lord

Lord, help me when I fall,
Push me on, Lord, when I stall;
Lord, lift me up when I'm down,
When I go the wrong way, turn me around.
Lord, if I begin to feel depressed,
Remind me of how much I'm blessed;
Chastise me, Lord, when I'm bad,
But comfort me, Lord, when I'm sad.
When I feel so alone as I stand,
Let me feel an angel holding my hand;
When the devil shows up to ruin my day,
Lord, help me rebuke him, send him on his way.
I want to serve you, dear Jesus, all I can,
But you already know that I'm just a man;
If it was just me, and me alone,
I could never make it, just my flesh and bone.
You said you would never forsake or leave me,
You are always there when I need Thee;
Thank you, Lord, for the gifts you give,
And thank you, Lord, for showing me how to live.

The Auction

The voice of the auctioneer,
Came from the speakers loud and clear;
He was speaking through a microphone,
Trying to sell an old telephone.
The bidding seemed to go real slow,
The price on the phone I knew would be low;
I had no interest in the old phone,
I had other interests of my own.
There on the table was a model ship,
One that I had at one time built;
The mahogany wood, the brass rails,
Two tall masts and snow-white sails.
Sitting in a glassed-in case,
With every part in perfect place;
Someone had stolen this little ship of mine,
But there it stood on the auction line.
I bid first as the bidding began,
And waited a moment to see how it ran;
The price went up as others wanted to buy,
But I finally got it though the price was high.
Now it's mine, sitting on a shelf,
I made it and bought it all by myself.

The Barber Shop

I walked into the barber shop,
My long, stringy hair looking like a mop;
I said to the barber, "Sir, what can you say,
Is the price of a haircut that I must pay?"
I caught his eye and saw him stare,
At the clothes I wore and my long, stringy hair;
"Ten dollars," he said, "I think will do.
Have a seat, and I'll soon be with you."
So I waited and waited until the day was past,
Finally it came my turn at last;
I sat down in the barber's chair,
And waited while he cut my hair.
When he finished, I sat still,
And asked again, "How much is my bill?"
"Twelve dollars," he said to me.
I said, "But sir, how can this be,
Twelve dollars now? This morning it was ten."
He said, "The cost of living has gone up since then."

The Bible

The Bible is a book of books authored by our God above,
Known to be God's Holy Word, it simply expresses God's mercy and love;
It tells us about sin and the plan of salvation,
And how the story should be told in every nation.
It tells us about how Jesus was crucified,
How He was nailed to a cross and there He died;
There are places that tell about His resurrection,
But He is coming again, it says in Revelation.
Judgment is coming some great day,
No mercy for those who rejected His way;
Believe in thine heart Christ died for you,
Repent of your sins is the thing to do.

The Bird

The bird was graceful as it glided along,
Landed in a tree and sang a song;
It really amazes me,
How a little bird seems so carefree.
I like to watch them fly through the sky,
And often wish that I could fly;
And sail about from place to place,
Ignoring this world's fast, hectic pace.

The Bridal Show

At a bridal extravaganza one day,
I saw all kinds of wedding things on display;
I saw would-be grooms standing everywhere,
With a glazed look, wondering, "What am I doing here?"
There were future brides of every shape and size,
With dreams in their heads and stars in their eyes;
They tried on tiaras and wedding gowns,
They looked at wedding cakes and heard music sounds.
The fashion show was really good,
With every model looking like a bride should;
They wore beautiful gowns with long-flowing trains,
Making some parents' bank account ache with pain.
A broad smile brightened every bride's face,
Looking forward to the time the wedding took place.

The Cattle Shed Event

The roof above was a cattle shed,
A feed trough was used for the baby's bed;
A pretty young girl was the child's mother,
At that time, the child had neither sister nor brother.
Mary was the young mother's name,
Chosen by God, she was found without shame;
The father was Joseph, a devout young man,
Whom God had chosen to carry out His plan.
Jesus was the name they gave this little child,
He grew up full of love; He was meek and mild;
Though Joseph was the father to most of the world,
It was really God who seeded the young girl.
This child was not just ordinary,
For God had spoken to Joseph and Mary;
This child was God's Holy Son,
Sent to earth as Redeemer for everyone.

The Country Road

The country road went winding along,
Bordered by trees large and strong;
On each side was a shallow ditch,
Where water stood still as black as pitch.
A car bounced along on the bumpy road,
Then came a truck with a heavy load;
This old road is traveled quite a bit,
It goes down near the river to the gravel pit.
The holes in the road have been patched before,
But every time I look, I know I see more.

The Dark Red Rose

The dark red rose is my favorite flower,
There's one in the kitchen and one near the shower;
Some are on the table in the dining room,
Some are still closed, some in full bloom.
The stems are long; the leaves are green,
One of the loveliest sights my eyes have seen;
I listen to the rose, a message is heard,
Though it cannot speak or say a word.
The red rose tells of a love divine,
God instilled in your heart and mine;
The petals are so sweet to smell,
No way could I miss the story they tell.
God's love is good, sweet, and pure,
In a world of confusion, His love is sure.

The Devil

The devil came to church today,
Trying to start a fight;
But I sent that devil on his way,
God's side is always right.
The devil always comes to church,
Trying hard to deceive;
The thing that seems to really hurt,
Is so many folks will believe.
The devil is good at telling lies,
He tells them all the time;
And before some people realize,
He's done messed up their mind.
Don't let the devil mislead you, friend,
Like he really wants to do;
Or you'll find out in the end,
He's got the best of you.

11/03/2004

The Difference

The difference between East and West,
Is like the difference between the worst and the best;
The difference between wrong and right,
Is as great as the difference between darkness and light.
The difference between Heaven and Hell,
Is like the difference between a tower and a well;
Heaven will be the home of those who repent,
Hell is the place where the wicked will be sent.
Jesus dying on the old rugged cross,
Makes all the difference between the saved and the lost;
The saved follow the path Jesus trod,
While the lost have turned their back on God.
In seeking eternal life, do you really know,
If you are going to heaven or to hell below?
If you want to go to heaven and not be among the lost,
Trust in Jesus now, He has already paid the cost.

10/1997

The First Easter

"Why seek ye the living among the dead?"
These are the words the holy angel said;
The tomb was empty; the sepulcher no longer His bed,
The cloth was folded that once covered His head.
"He has arisen!" they heard the angle say,
"Go tell His disciples; hasten on your way."
Mary Magdalene was happy on that bright morn,
Her spirits were lifted; her heart no longer torn.
The wages of sin have been fully paid,
For all who trust in Him, they shall surely be saved;
Who is this one who has conquered the grave,
Defeated Satan and has the power to save?
Jesus Christ, our Savior and King!
Let us spread the word and His praises sing.

03/1998

The Forest Fire

The fire was raging,
The flames leaped high;
The forest was burning,
May creatures would die.
The smoke was thick,
It smothered my breath;
To stay here long,
Could surely mean death.
The roar of the flames,
And the burning smell;
Go with the heat,
In this man-made hell.
A tossed cigarette,
Is how it all began;
A thoughtless act,
Of a careless man.

The Men's Restroom

Outside the door of the men's restroom,
Hoping the guy inside will come out soon;
Impatiently waiting in a nervous sweat,
If he doesn't hurry up, I'm gonna be wet.
Nature seems to have a way to make us want to go,
And then cause us to wait;
We cross our legs and wiggle and squirm,
Trying to look casual, but feeling like a worm.
The man comes out; I step in the door,
The room is filthy, water on the floor;
That's the life of a traveling man,
You answer nature's call whenever you can.

The Mermaid

She looked so lovely with long golden hair,
And pretty blue eyes and a face light and fair;
Her body was covered with fish-like scales,
And instead of feet she had a fish tail.
The ocean was her place called home,
With plenty of room to play and to roam;
She came to the surface for a breath of air,
And from the ship I saw her there.
She swam about there in the sea,
And smiled and waved and flirted with me.

The Mountain

The mountain stood majestically very large and very high,
Its base was very broad; its peak pointed to the sky;
An old man once lived on the mountainside,
There he was born and there he died.
The mountain was to that man the only place he knew as home,
And on its broad, wooded sides is where often he would roam;
From the lofty mountaintop to the valley far below,
There were no secrets this mountain held that the old man didn't know.
He hunted through the forest for his daily meat,
And in a little garden he grew his food to eat;
This mountain was the only home the old man ever knew,
He spent his life there on its side among the trees the mountain grew.

The New School

I watched the men at work building a new school,
They seemed to be very skilled at using every kind of tool;
The cement was poured and leveled; the men were working rather hard,
A grader too, was moving dirt, smoothing out the ground of the yard.
The structure was of solid steel; brick was added to the outside then,
And when the roof was finished, the building was weathered in;
The classrooms had large windows and pretty tile on the floor,
A telephone in every room and a fire alarm by every door.
I wonder what the children will be who come to learn at this school,
Maybe doctors, lawyers, ministers, politicians, and perhaps there will be a few fools;
Many will take advantage of what the school has to give,
While others will probably just exist, not ever learning how to really live.

The New Year

The old year is past,
Its days are all gone;
Now it's time to look ahead,
As time continues on.
We turn the calendar page,
A new time is here;
The past is all history,
It's a brand-new year.
Will it bring more war and violence,
Turbulence and crime;
Or will it bring us happiness and peace,
With the passing of time?
No one knows what the future may hold,
But we'll see the days as they unfold.

The Passing Of Time

The old year is gone; it's a thing of the past,
The new year finally is here at last;
The old year goes down in history,
What's in the new year, we all wait to see.
As the days go by from morn to morn,
Some people will die and others be born;
Time is so short in many, many ways,
Makes it hard to keep up with the passing of days.
Some days are filled with joy, happiness, and cheer,
While others are long, sad, and so drear;
The days may come and the days may go,
But God will always be in control, I know.

The Pawn Shop

I walked into a pawn shop one day,
And saw all the things there on display;
There were guitars and guns and many things more,
Watches and rings and many tools galore.
I can buy what I want if I pay the cost,
But what I may get, someone else has lost;
If you need money, they have it to loan,
On anything of value that you may own.

The Small Cabinet Shop

Power saws are humming,
You can hear the blades whine;
The planer is running,
You can smell the fresh pine.
The dust hangs thick,
In this small shop;
It will make you sick,
If it soon doesn't stop.
A living I must try to make,
As I breathe this pollution;
It's all for the family's sake,
But there must be a solution.

The Small Town Cafe

In Cleveland, Texas,
There is a fine café;
The name of this place,
Is called, "Yesterday."
There are memories,
Of things in the past;
Of musicians and singers;
And movie casts.
The jukebox plays,
Songs from back then;
And you sit at the table,
And reflect back when.
Elvis and the Beatles,
Were going real strong;
Their music was played,
All night and day long.
You can sit upstairs,
Or down below;
But there's one thing for sure,
That you will soon know.
The food is good,
And the service is too;
The staff is friendly,
As they try to please you.

Time

The days come,
The days go;
Some fly by,
Others are slow.
Time is present,
Future and past;
Some things come to stay,
Others never last.
The shifting of sand,
The passing of time;
Many thoughts come and go,
Through my mind.
Time is an element,
We all must endure;
We have thoughts that are bad,
And thoughts that are pure.
Time can be valuable,
Time can be cheap;
Time can make us happy,
Or time can make us weep.

To Build A Church

If I should want to build a church,
Where should I start?
Should I buy boards and nails,
Or try to reach the peoples' heart?

If building a church was my dream,
And ultimately was my goal;
Maybe I should not start with a hammer and nails,
But first win a lost and dying soul.

They say the foundation is the most important part,
It must be firm and strong from the very start;
The foundation that I am thinking of,
Is made of prayer and Christian love.

To Start The Day

I like to sing God's songs,
And read the Bible too;
When everything else is going wrong,
That seems the thing to do.
I often get on my knees and pray,
And talk to Jesus there;
There's nothing better to make my day,
Than a little while in prayer.
Sing and pray and study God's Word,
Be ready to face the day;
When Jesus speaks, make sure you hear,
Everything He has to say.

Today

Yesterday, today was tomorrow,
Some days bring happiness; others bring only sorrow;
The days seem to hasten by,
No matter if we laugh or even if we cry.
Each morning when I awake,
I lay there wondering which road I will take;
Will this be a good one,
Filled with happiness and joy and pleasure and fun?
Or will things suddenly go bad,
Making today the worst that I have ever had?
I know not what lies ahead,
Before the day is over I may even be dead;
So as I travel along my way,
I will seek God's guidance throughout this long day.

Tracy

Her hair was blonde; her smile was sweet,
She looked so good from her head to her feet;
I wanted to know her and be her friend,
And have some time with her to spend.
Now I know her and know her well,
She's my special friend, I am happy to tell.
Sometimes I see her and we sit and talk,
But I wish I could take her for a walk;
On a trek through the mall or a trail in the wood,
Just to be with her all that I could.
The clothes she wears can be plain or lacy,
But she will always be my friend named Tracy.

Troubled World

The world is full of mystery,
And things that seem so strange to me;
Humanity can't seem to get along,
Pollution is destroying earth's ozone.
The rain forest is thin; oxygen is low,
The world is burning out ever so slow;
Evil lurks in mankind's heart,
Set out to tear the world apart.
Greed and envy brings on hate,
Causing a rise in the crime rate;
Storms occurring in every land,
Wars over things I can't understand.
I wonder if we are really free,
Or just what might be our destiny;
Are we heading for our final doom?
I guess we'll know sometime soon.

War

The war was raging; smoked filled the air,
Guns were firing; bullets flying everywhere;
The bursting of a hand grenade,
A wounded soldier crying for aid.
There seemed to be no rest from the fight,
As the battle went on through day and night;
Many young men out there would die,
Never really knowing or understanding why.

Wendi

I know a little girl,
Her name is Wendi Lenz;
She is a sweet little girl,
And one of my favorite friends.
She is like a heavenly angel,
Sent from God above;
To bring to her Mom and Dad,
A light of joy and love.
She reminds me of my daughter,
Going back many years in time;
Who brought joy and happiness,
In the life of my wife and mine.

This little poem was written for the daughter of a former Pastor of mine.
Little Wendi wanted me to write a poem just for her.

When We Were Wed

There she stood in a long, white veil,
Looking so pretty, though a little pale;
Wearing a beautiful white wedding gown,
She was known by everybody in town.
Her dress had a train real long,
The orchestra was playing our favorite song;
The maid of honor stood by her side,
Her mother sat on the front row and cried.
Her father was the one to give her away,
He was dressed real nice on this special day.
My good friend was standing there,
He was my best man and willing to share;
In the joy and happiness of this special event,
This would for him be a time well spent.
The minister stood straight and serene,
The calmest person in this whole scene;
Well, the wedding is over, the people are gone,
My new wife and I are going away alone.
Oh Boy! She's my bride!
I feel her warmth when she's by my side;
Oh Boy! I love her so much!
My heart leaps when I feel her touch.

Winter Storm

I could hear the howling of the cold north wind,
I thought to myself, "This will never end."
The snow was heavily falling, the tree limbs bent,
From the raging winter storm through the day done spent.
The darkness now has chased away the light,
But the storm still rages on into the night.

Work

My cup is empty, coffee is all gone,
Time for me to arise and start moving on;
To earn more money, I must go off to work,
To buy more food and coffee to perk.
It's work, work all the time,
To buy food for energy, I can't save a dime;
It's food for energy; it's money for food,
It's working for the money that puts me in this mood.

You Outshine Them All

In life's overall plan,
God has someone for every woman and man;
Some of them are short; some of them are tall,
But, Baby, you are the one that outshines them all.
Some people are large; some people are small,
But, Baby, you are the one that outshines them all.
Some people seem to fly while others seem to crawl,
But, Baby, you are the one that outshines them all.

Lorraine and me

My Three children, Ellen, Tim and Steve

Me and Lynn at my 85th birthday party at North Cleveland Baptist church Fellowship hall, Cleveland Texas 2013

My three step children (Lynn's children)
David, Theresa, John

My wife Lynn

Lynn and me shortly after we married

Me in my friend's Highway 59 Music store.
The guitar was a birthday gift to me from Dale Bianchi,
owner of the music store.

Me and my Harley. 1948 – I was 20 years old

Me at 9 months

Lorraine at the time we were married in 1948

**Me at age 18 years old
- In U.S. Navy**

Me in diving suit going over the side during diving practice at Key West, Florida, 1947

Rev. Gordon Langford

Table of Contents-Songs

A Better Day 131
A Fisher Of Men 132
A Million Times Is Not Enough 133
A Place Of My Own 134
Along For The Ride 135
An Old Man's Journey 136
Ashes To Ashes 138
Be A Winner 139
Best To Serve Jesus 141
Between Heaven And Hell 143
Born Again 144
Broken Home 145
Built With Nail-Scarred Hands 146
Cross To A Crown 147
Final Trip 148
Forgiven 149
God's Children Were Praying For Me 150
Have You Talked To The Savior 151
He Died For Me 153
He Had To Make Everything New 154
He Will Make Me Whole 155
He's Here With Me 156
He's Living In Me 157

Hear Me When I Talk	158
Heaven	160
Highway To Heaven	161
I Don't Know	163
I Need Jesus To Hold My Hand	164
I Trusted Jesus	165
I Want To Shout And Sing	166
I'm Going Home	167
I'm Gonna Be Gone	168
I'm No Longer The Same	169
I'm Waiting 'Till I Get There	170
If Jesus Went On Vacation	171
It's Christmas Time	172
Jesus And Me	173
Jesus Came Looking For Me	174
Judgement	175
Knocking At The Door	177
Life's Choices	178
Lift Him Up	179
Make Me A Temple	181
Mary's Lamb	182
New Point Of View	183
Nothing's Wrong With Me	184
Now I Live For Jesus	186
Oh, What A Savior	187
On Eagles Wings	188

Our Savior Lives	189
Rocking Alone In An Old Rocking Chair (2 Verses)	190
Sing About Jesus	192
Sinner, Please Don't Wait	193
Take Jesus	194
The Bird In The Window	195
The Brighter Side	197
The Change	198
The Devil Ain't A Gonna Bother Me	200
The Dream	201
The Good Shepherd	203
The Sky Is The Limit	204
Walk With Me, Jesus	205
Walking On High Ground	206
Walking On The Water Of The River Of Life	207
What People See	208
When God Calls My Name	209
When It's Gospel Singing Time In Heaven	210
When The Rooster Crowed	211
When The Wind Blows	212
Where The Milk And Honey Flows	213
Will You Readily Grasp Him By The Hand	214
Between Your Heart And Mine	215
Fonder, More Fonder	216
Headaches And Heartaches	217
I Just Can't Get Away From You	219

I'm In Love With You 220
No Money 221
Nothing To Do - (After Surgery) 222
The Blue Valley Waltz 223

A Better Day

(1)
This old world with all its troubles, its wars, and its woes,
Will be left here behind when it comes time to go;
Jesus will be coming in the twinkling of an eye,
Then all of His children will meet Him in the sky.
(Chorus)
There's a better day a coming by and by,
And that day I know is drawing nigh.
At the sound of Gabriel's trumpet,
When Christ appears in the sky,
I'll know a better day is coming by and by.
(2)
The graves will be opened; the dead in Christ shall rise,
To go to be with Jesus at that meeting in the sky;
All the lost ones will be left puzzled here behind,
Not knowing what has happened; not a Christian can they find.

(2013)

A Fisher Of Men

(1)
Jesus was walking along the seashore,
Peter was mending his net as he oft had before;
Jesus stopped and said, "I need someone to send.
Come, follow me, and I'll make you a fisher of men."
(Chorus)
Fishers of men, be a fisher of men,
So many people are lost in a sea of sin;
Go rescue them and bring them in,
Just follow Jesus and be a fisher of men.
(2)
Peter dropped his net and away he went,
Not knowing just what it all meant;
But he went along with Jesus and then,
Soon he became a fisher of men.
(3)
The harvest is great, but the laborers are few,
Jesus was talking to me and to you;
Go through the world and bring them in,
Get busy and be a fisher of men.

04/20/2008

A Million Times Is Not Enough

(1)
As I look around me, Lord, I see you everywhere,
I see you in the sky above, and I feel you in the air;
You're always with me, Lord, in everything I do,
Lord, a million times is not enough to say I love you.
(Chorus)
Lord, a million times is not enough to say I love you,
Or to thank you, Lord, for the many things that you always do;
Counting all my blessings, Lord, I find there is no end,
In knowing all my weakness, Lord, on you I must depend.
(2)
You are my strength in weakness, Lord, my comfort in strife,
You are my healer, Lord, in the illnesses of life;
When the storms arise, Lord, you're there to see me through,
Oh, a million times is not enough to say I love you.
(3)
When I pass through the door of death, Lord, I know you'll be there,
With open arms and a welcome smile, in heaven so fair;
There will be no more troubles, Lord, for me to go through,
Lord, a million times is not enough to say I love you.

12/24/2011

A Place Of My Own

(1)
There's a mansion for me,
Where I long to be.
It's prepared by Jesus' own hand.
There's gold on the floor,
And pearl on the door.
Yes, heaven will be so grand.
(Chorus)
Oh, how I long,
For my heavenly home,
Far beyond the sky.
It's a place of my own,
And I'll soon be gone,
To be in that sweet by and by.
(2)
There God is the light,
No darkness, no night.
Everything is so peaceful there.
No devil to fight;
I'll soon take flight,
To that meeting in the air.
(3)
In that wonderful place,
I'll see Jesus' face,
When I reach heaven's bright shore.
With a new voice,
Around His throne I'll rejoice,
In heaven I'll live evermore.

Along For The Ride

I'm just an old man along for the ride.
Wherever my wife goes, I'll be by her side;
Whatever she says, that I will abide,
After all, I'm just along for the ride.

Many years ago, my first wife died,
God gave me another to keep me occupied;
When I go to heaven, a wife on each side,
I'll tell St. Peter I'm just along for the ride.

06/24/2013

An Old Man's Journey

(1)
This old world has much to offer,
Some good and some bad;
I've seen my share,
I've been happy and I've been sad.
I've been in the valley,
And on the mountain so high;
I've sailed on the ocean,
And I've flown through the sky.
(Chorus)
Now, I'm just an old man,
Getting closer to home,
As I travel this road of life that I'm on.
The years are getting shorter,
The days go by so fast;
Most of my living is all in the past.
(2)
I've often been lonely and sometimes depressed,
Then I went to my Lord and found how much I'd been blessed;
Jesus has been with me as I went through it all,
We laughed some and cried some, but we never did fall.
(3)
This road has been long and rough often times,
But it's getting a bit smoother as I near the end of the line;
In heaven they say the streets are pure gold,
It's a place where the body will never grow old.
(4)
My earthly life will someday be gone,

Then I'll start life eternal in my heavenly home;
There will be no more suffering, no sorrow, nor sin,
I'll be happy there forever in a life with no end.

01/29/2013

Ashes To Ashes

(1)
People are funny, I've heard it said,
No plans for the soul when the body is dead;
Seems right to me to trust God's plan,
Prepare for the future here while you can.
(Chorus)
Ashes to ashes, dust to dust,
Wood to rot, iron to rust;
Body to die, but not the soul,
Death to life, in Christ made whole.
(2)
I'm gonna live forever, though the body may die,
Soul will be with Jesus in the sweet by and by;
Some people may guess, but for me I know,
When I breathe my last breath, just where I will go.
(3)
Things in this world will soon decay,
Bodies will return to the earth and clay;
If you love Christ, serve Him every day,
There's nothing to fear when death comes your way.

09/24/2005

Be A Winner

(1)
David went to the camp to take his brothers some food,
There he challenged the giant who was in a mean mood;
"You come to me with shield and a sword,
I come to you in the name of the Lord."
The giant laughed and said, "You're only a boy,
With nothing in your hands but a little child's toy."
The battle was fought and the little boy won,
He put the enemy on the run!
(Chorus)
There are battles to fight in this world we live in,
No matter the problem, we know we can win;
With God leading us all the way,
We can overcome Satan day by day.
(2)
Elijah challenged the false prophets one day,
"To hear from your gods, why don't you pray?"
They prayed and prayed and began to weep;
Elijah said, "Your gods must all be asleep."
They gritted their teeth and fell on their face,
But their idols were silent there in that place;
From their false gods they never heard a sound,
Elijah prayed to the Lord, and the fire came down!
(3)
Peter and John preached to the crowd,
They preached very hard and they preached very loud;
The Pharisees said, "You must not preach."
Peter said, "I can't stop; there are souls to reach."

Be A Winner

They were thrown into a dusty jail cell,
They kept singing and preaching as though all was well;
The angel came and opened the door,
They went out and preached to the people some more!
(4)
When Joshua came to Jericho,
God said, "There's something that you need to know.
You and the people must march around that wall,
Then blow your trumpets and watch it fall."
Joshua listened to God, and then he obeyed,
He carried out the plan that God had made;
The victory was his, the city was won,
Because they listened to God, and then it was done.

05/03/2001

Best To Serve Jesus

(Recitation Form)

Are you a chosen disciple,
Like Mark, Luke, and John?
Are you an active Christian,
Or are you a still one?

Are you living for Jesus,
Do you put forth your all?
Do you pray every day,
Do you put forth your all?

Do you try to help others,
Do you show them the way,
To become a real Christian?
Do you daily pray?

Are you living a clean life,
Just like Jesus did;
Or do you have sinful secrets,
That you would rather keep hid?

Do you often go places,
Where you'd rather not be found?
Do you heed the devil's temptations,
Or do you turn them down?

Old Satan will temp you,

Best To Serve Jesus

And he'll lead you astray;
It's best to serve Jesus,
And live the Christian way.

Between Heaven And Hell

(1)
On the cross, Jesus was crucified,
Beaten and bleeding, His life slipped away;
Paying the debt for our sins when He died,
On that cross one sad, dark day.
(Chorus)
Somewhere between heaven and hell,
A cross stood on a hill;
God's Son was crucified there,
For the price of our sins, He paid the bill.
(2)
A tomb was carved in a mountain of stone,
A place of rest for the dead;
Jesus was put there and left all alone,
With only a napkin placed over His head.
(3)
The empty tomb later was found,
No sign of Jesus, as they looked all around;
Jesus has arisen, He's alive and well,
He's now my Lord; He saved me from hell.
(Finish)
Somewhere between heaven and hell,
A cross stood on a hill;
With arms outstretched, Jesus hung there,
"Father, forgive them," was His dying prayer.

05/12/2011

Born Again

(1)
From my mother's womb, I entered this world,
Darkness and sin around me unfurled;
Satan was there to take control,
To ruin my life and destroy my soul.
(Chorus) V.1 - But, V.2 - Now, V.3 - Yes
But I'm free! I'm free!
From what I used to be.
I no longer live a life of sin.
Praise God! Praise God!
One day I found Jesus,
Then I was born again.
(2)
I struggled through many long years,
And seemed to shed a million tears;
The devil had me in his hand,
'Till I asked Jesus to take command.
(3)
I was born again to serve my Savior,
To do His will and seek His favor;
No longer bound by sin's strong cord,
I live for Jesus now and praise the Lord.

10/23/2005

Broken Home

(Chorus)
Storm clouds are gathering all about me,
Since you said goodbye and went away;
Seems a storm of blues surround me,
Since I received your farewell note yesterday.

(1)
You said you weren't leaving me for another,
For really you love me deep inside;
But you cannot live with a cheater,
For you say that you've already tried.

(2)
I'm sorry that I cheated on you, dear,
And yesterday I made a vow;
That I will never do you wrong again, dear,
If I can only get you back somehow.

(3)
These blues will never leave me, my darling,
Until you decide to come back;
But I guess it took a jolt like this, dear,
To put my heart on the right track.

Built With Nail-Scarred Hands

(1)
Jesus said He was going to heaven,
To prepare a place for me;
With hands that were nail-scarred,
On the cross of Calvary.
(Chorus)
Oh, the nail-scarred hands of Jesus,
Built a place for me;
With the skills of a master carpenter,
Built to last for eternity.
(2)
He made the walls of jasper,
Pure gold He put on the floor;
No lights in my mansion are needed,
There will be no locks on my door.
(3)
Someday I know He'll be coming,
Although I know not when;
But when my home is completed,
I'll be ready to move right in.
(4)
I shall live in this mansion forever,
All of God's glory I'll share;
In this new house that Christ built,
It will be so wonderful there.

10/02/2003

Cross To A Crown

(1)
Jesus came from the tomb where His body had laid,
When the wages of sin on the cross had been paid;
Jesus left this earth in victory,
He defeated Satan at Calvary.
(Chorus)
From a cross to a crown was the path Jesus trod,
From a sinful world to the throne of God;
Thirty-three years to the cross where He laid His life down,
Three days from the cross He went to His crown.
(2)
It was on the cross He bled and died,
He suffered so much when He was crucified;
He carried the cross 'till He stumbled and fell,
He suffered the torment to save us from hell.
(3)
He was headed for the cross when He left the womb,
He was headed for the crown when He left the tomb;
Jesus often said, "I am going away,
But I shall return some glorious day!"
(Tag)
When Jesus ascended, He was glory bound.
He went from His cross all the way to His crown!

03/27/2003

Final Trip

All God's children are going away,
Going away, going away;
All God's children are going away,
On that rapture day.

We're gonna meet Jesus in the air,
In the air, in the air;
We're gonna meet Jesus in the air,
All God's children gonna be there.

Gonna see Jesus face to face,
Face to face, face to face;
Gonna see Jesus face to face,
In that heavenly place.

Jesus gonna take us to our heavenly home,
Heavenly home, heavenly home;
Jesus gonna take us to our heavenly home,
One that will be our very own.

Forgiven

(1)
Jesus looked at the crowd as He hung on the cross,
He saw a world that was hopelessly lost;
"Father forgive them," was His final prayer,
But the people ignored Him; they seemed not to care.
(Chorus)
I am forgiven for all the wrongs I have done,
I've been forgiven by God's only Son;
My life has been changed, my sins washed away,
By the shed blood of Jesus on the cross that day.
(2)
My life was full of evil and sin,
Worldly pleasure was my lifestyle back then;
One day I went to church, I heard the preacher say,
"Give your life to Jesus, He'll change you today."

02/25/2004

God's Children Were Praying For Me

(Chorus)
God's children were praying for me,
God's children were praying for me;
God heard their prayer away back there,
God's children were praying for me.
(1)
Time went by from months into years,
My father prayed and shed many tears;
God sent His Spirit to beckon to me,
I turned to Jesus, and now I'm free.
(2)
My father rejoiced; the angels did too,
When I cried, "Lord Jesus, I believe in You."
When Jesus came and saved my soul,
He forgave my sins and made me whole.
(3)
God touched my heart and called me to preach,
There are many lost souls He wants me to reach;
He said, "Tell them the things I've done for you.
I will do the same thing for them too."

11/19/1999

Have You Talked To The Savior

(1)
Have you talked to the Savior today?
Did you take time out to pray?
Did you tell Him you love Him,
That you want to serve Him?
Have you talked to the Savior today?
(Chorus)
He said, "I'll never leave you,
Nor will I forsake you;
I'll always be faithful and true.
Follow me is my call,
Give me your all;
I'll always be there for you."
(2)
Have you listened to the Savior today?
Did you hear what He had to say?
Have you done what He asked you,
All the things He said do?
Have you listened to the Savior today?
(3)
Have you walked with the Savior today?
Were you with Him every step of the way?
Did you let Him lead you,
Bear your burdens for you?
Have you walked with the Savior today?
(4)
Oh, I felt the Savior today,
I felt Him in so many ways.

Have You Talked To The Savior

When I wanted to cry,
He brushed the tears from my eye.
Yes, I felt the Savior today.
(Tag)
Have you been with Jesus today?

09/10/2004

He Died For Me

(1)
He fed the multitude there on the mountain,
He shared the water of life with the woman at the fountain;
He walked on the water of Galilee,
But most of all, He died for me.
(Chorus)
Jesus died for me on Calvary,
His rich, red blood set me free;
Free from the bondage of all my sin,
He gave me peace and joy and love within.
(2)
One bright day, He gave the blind man new sight,
Among the tombs of Gadara, He made the maniac right;
He made the dumb to speak and the blind to see,
But most of all, He died for me.
(3)
One glad day, He gave Lazarus new life,
He healed the sick woman and took away her strife;
There in the storm He calmed the wild sea,
But most of all, He died for me.
(4)
At the wedding, He turned the water into wine,
He proved in the temple that He is divine;
He heard the cry of the thief as He hung on the tree,
But most of all, He died for me.

He Had To Make Everything New

(Start)
When Jesus moved into my heart,
He had so much to do;
It wasn't hard to find a place to start,
He had to make everything new.
(1)
He cleaned out the closet; He scrubbed the floor.
Every old sin He would toss it,
Right out my heart's door,
He had to make everything new.
(2)
He painted the walls with blood of His own,
To cover the stains of my sin;
It all had to be done before He could move in,
He had to make everything new.
(3)
It was a job, I regret to say,
My sins could be found everywhere;
They were scattered in disarray,
He cleaned them out; now His spirit lives there.
He had to make everything new.

He Will Make Me Whole

(1)
I have traveled this world, seen many sights,
I've seen the beauty of day and the evils of night;
I've done many things, both good and bad,
But deep in my soul, I feel so sad.
(Chorus)
If I may but touch the garment of Jesus,
I know that He will save my soul;
If I may but touch the hem of His garment,
He will surely make me whole.
(2)
I press through the crowd of people about me,
But none of them know what I really need;
Jesus is near; He's passing by,
And I know that He will hear my cry.
(3)
I'm in good health and I've been to school,
I try to live by the golden rule;
My friends all think I'm doing just fine,
But there's an empty spot in this soul of mine.

He's Here With Me

(1)
I never walked beside the river Jordan,
I never saw Mount Calvary;
I never felt the scars in the hands of Jesus,
But I know, yes I know, He's here with me.
(Chorus)
When I am on the mountain, I know that He is there,
When I am in the valley, I can feel His loving care;
This one thing I surely know,
Jesus is with me wherever I go.
(2)
I never saw inside the empty tomb,
I wasn't there when He calmed the sea;
I never ate when He fed the thousands,
But I know, yes I know, He's here with me.
(3)
I never saw Him raise the dead,
I never heard the dumb man speak;
I wasn't there when He walked on the water,
But I know, yes I know, He's here with me.
(4)
I wasn't around when He healed the sick,
Nor when He set the maniac free;
I never heard His prayers in the garden,
But I know, yes I know, He's here with me.

He's Living In Me

(1)
With thorns on His head, nails in His feet,
He asked God's forgiveness for you and for me;
His head hung low as He breathed His last breath,
He paid for my sins in the torments of death.
(Chorus)
Jesus died there on Calvary,
Yet He's now alive and living in me;
Praise God, Praise God, now I am set free,
For Jesus is alive and well and living in me.
(2)
They placed Jesus in a borrowed tomb,
It was only temporary; He'd be leaving there soon;
Three days later, or there about,
Angels moved the stone and Jesus came out.
(3)
Am I worthy to have such a guest,
As I go through life while doing my best;
In times of darkness when it's hard to see,
Jesus is there; He's living in me.

09/16/2007

Hear Me When I Talk

(1)
Sinner, won't you listen?
Hear me when I talk.
Sinner, can you hear me?
Hear me when I talk.
I want to tell you about a Savior,
Who died on Calvary's cross.
Hear me when I talk.
(2)
Sinner, are you listening?
Hear me when I talk.
Sinner, do you hear me?
Hear me when I talk.
The wages of sin are death,
But Jesus paid the cost.
Hear me when I talk.
(3)
Sinner, I hope you hear me.
Hear me when I talk.
Sinner, pay attention.
Hear me when I talk.
This life will soon be over,
And death on you will call.
Hear me when I talk.
(4)
Sinner, I know you hear me.
Hear me when I talk.
Sinner, it's time to listen.

Hear me when I talk.
Don't go without the Savior,
Better give Jesus your all.

07/28/2009

Heaven

(1)
I want to walk the streets of Gory,
I want to walk the streets paved with gold;
I want to see the mansion of Moses,
And of all the Saints of old.
I want to see the face of Jesus,
I want to hear the angels sing;
I want to join their heavenly chorus,
And let my Hosannas ring.
(Chorus)
Yes, Jesus prepared a mansion in Glory,
He prepared one just for me;
He said He's coming back for me,
That where He is there I may be.
(2)
They tell me that heaven is a place of beauty,
They tell me I'll find no sorrow there;
They tell me in heaven I'll be happy,
There will be rejoicing everywhere.
The bright light there will forever be shining,
Coming from God's great white throne;
I want to walk with Jesus, my Savior,
And have that mansion all my own.

Highway To Heaven

(Chorus)
I'm traveling the highway to heaven,
Serving my Lord every day;
I'm paving the road I leave behind me,
With the deeds I do along the way.
(1)
I started my journey to heaven,
Holding on to my Savior's hand;
He guided my footsteps so gently,
Though there were so many shells in the sand.
The highway is not easy to heaven,
It's narrow and not often trod;
Those who travel the road to heaven,
Must travel by the roadmap of God.
(2)
When I gave my heart to Jesus,
He gave me salvation so free;
He put me on the road to heaven,
Where I could live with Him eternally.
The world is floundering about me,
Without Jesus holding their hand;
They are traveling down the wrong highway,
And they just don't seem to understand.
(3)
There are those who are watching me,
As I travel heaven's highway;
I must not fall or stumble,
And cause someone else to go astray.

Highway To Heaven

I must let them know this about me,
That what I am I will always stay;
And try not to mislead them,
As I travel heaven's highway.

03/15/1999

I Don't Know

(Chorus)
When Jesus is coming again, I don't know,
But when He comes, I'm ready to go;
I don't know when His coming will be,
But when He comes, He'll be coming for me.
(1)
He says in His Word He's coming again,
All His children, He will gather them in;
He's coming to take us to our heavenly home,
We will live in a mansion of our very own.
(2)
I don't know if you are saved or lost,
You should know Jesus paid the cost;
He went on a mountain called Calvary,
Where He died on the cross for you and me.
(3)
Believe on Jesus; put your trust in Him,
He will save your soul from all your sin;
Let the spirit within you grow and grow,
But why Jesus loves us, I really don't know.

10/26/2001

I Need Jesus To Hold My Hand

(1)
Hurricanes and tornadoes, earthquakes in the land,
There're fires and floods that get out of hand;
There're rebellious children and parents with no care,
The downfall of mankind can be seen everywhere.
(Chorus)
I need Jesus to hold my hand,
I find it difficult just to stand;
Nature's in turmoil and so is man,
I need Jesus to hold my hand.
(2)
Life of the multitudes is full of evil and sin,
They don't even know the trouble they're in;
The Lord is returning most any day,
To seek out His children and take them away.
(Tag)
I must tell others and do all I can,
But I need Jesus to hold my hand.

09/24/2005

I Trusted Jesus

(1)
A thousand times or more,
I cried as I paced the floor;
So many problems, no answer to,
Which way to turn or what to do.
(Chorus)
Then I trusted Jesus; I made Him my Lord,
He changed me as He promised in His Word;
I no longer worry; I no longer grieve,
Everything changed in my life when I first believed.
(2)
All of the answers I once thought I knew,
Through the storms of life, I'd make it through;
But my burdens grew heavy, and I was so weak,
Life became weary; it looked so bleak.
(3)
Then I heard Jesus speak to me,
"Let me take your burdens, I'll set you free.
Give me your troubles; I'll bear them for you.
Through the storms of life, I'll see you through."

08/18/1998

I Want To Shout And Sing

(1)
Way out there on the old hillside,
They took Jesus, and there He died;
But from the grave my Savior came.
He was God's only Son,
The battle with death He has won;
He's my Lord, and I just praise His name.
(Chorus)
Lift me up; let me stand,
I want to see that glory land;
I want to see my Lord and King.
I want to stand and jump with joy,
Like a child with a newfound toy;
I just want to shout, shout and sing.
(2)
He has gone to heave above,
But He still reaches down with His love;
Seeking to save those lost in sin.
I love His blessings, and I want some more,
As I stand by heaven's door;
And the Lord beckons me to come on in.
(3)
Won't you listen to what I say,
Look to Jesus when He comes your way;
Leave your sin behind and follow Him.
The wages of sin is a terrible cost,
Are you saved or are you lost?
Jesus will forgive you all your sin.

I'm Going Home

(Chorus)
I'm going home, home at last,
Heaven's ahead; the world's in the past;
I'll see Jesus there on His golden throne,
Yes, finally I know I'm going home.
(1)
I've lived in this world so corrupted with sin,
I've seen many things; many places I've been;
This world is full of trouble and woe,
I'm leaving it soon; it's my time to go.
(2)
I'll never die as the world may guess,
I'm just moving on to a new address;
Don't weep for me when I'm gone,
Rejoice for me; I'm going home.
(3)
When I step through death's open door,
I'll be passing over to heaven's shore;
Make your plans now to come see me,
When you pass from time into eternity.

10/14/2006

I'm Gonna Be Gone

I'm gonna be gone; I'm gonna be gone,
I'm gonna leave this world alone;
You'll look for me, but I'll be gone,
Yes, one of these days, I'm gonna be gone.
(1)
There's another place I want to be,
There are saints of God I want to see;
I want to go there to my heavenly home,
One of these days, I'm gonna be gone.
(2)
God has a new place prepared for me,
And that is where I want to be;
I know now that it won't be long,
'Till the time will come and I'll be gone.
(3)
When I get there, I will rejoice,
I'll sing His praises with a brand-new voice;
I'll join the angels in their song,
Yes, it'll be soon I'm gonna be gone.
(4)
On the streets of gold with that heavenly band,
I'll praise my Lord and clap my hands;
I'll sing and shout around God's throne,
It won't be long 'till I'll be gone.

I'm No Longer The Same

(1)
Do you know Jesus; have you trusted Him?
Has He brightened your life when all seemed so dim?
Do you believe in Jesus deep down in your heart?
Have you given Him your life complete in every part?
(Chorus)
Jesus smiled at me; He smiled at me,
He said He loves me; Jesus loves me;
I can't understand; I just can't see,
For I'm so unworthy; I lived in sin.
In my darkest hour, all hope was gone,
The Lord Jesus came; He came to me;
Then He touched me, a gentle touch,
I'm no longer the same.
(2)
You may think that Jesus has everything.
Does He have your heart; have you been redeemed?
Freed from the world of bondage and sin,
Have you opened your heart and let Him come in?
(3)
Jesus bought you a mansion on heaven's bright shore,
Where you may someday go to dwell forevermore;
He paid with His blood at Mount Calvary,
The price was high for Him, but free for you and me.

11/16/1999

I'm Waiting 'Till I Get There

(1)
I read about a beautiful heaven,
I sing about amazing grace;
I feel the presence of Jesus,
I dream of seeing His face.

(Chorus)
But I'll wait until you call me, dear Jesus,
I'm waiting 'till I get there;
To dwell in that wonderful mansion,
In that beautiful heaven so fair.

(2)
His amazing grace has saved me,
Through the blood shed on Calvary's tree;
By faith I reached up for Him,
In love He reached down for me.

(3)
There are many questions to be answered,
About things I want to know;
But I'll ask them when I see Jesus,
The One that I love so.

05/29/2009

If Jesus Went On Vacation

(1)
If Jesus took a vacation,
Where would it be;
With no one to turn to,
And to take care of me?
If Jesus went on vacation,
My world would fall apart;
Trying to make it,
With just an empty heart.
(Chorus)
But Jesus never takes time off,
And never leaves us all alone;
To fight Satan single-handed,
And struggle on our own.
I can do all things through Christ,
Who strengthens me;
If I just have faith the size,
Of a tiny mustard seed.
(2)
If I knew that in heaven,
Jesus wasn't there;
Who could I talk to,
When I bend my knees in prayer?
If Jesus went on vacation,
And could not be found;
Satan would have a party,
And sin much more abound.

It's Christmas Time

(1)
Jesus was born in a cattle shed,
With a feed trough for a cradle and hay for a bed;
The animals were all standing there,
They could feel the excitement filling the air.
(Chorus)
It's Christmas time! It's Christmas time!
Joy fills the air;
People are celebrating His birth,
Almost everywhere.
(2)
The star was shining; the angels were singing,
The shepherds were on their way;
To worship this little newborn King,
Who lay there on the hay.
(3)
Jesus was born in a borrowed shed,
He was buried in a borrowed grave;
For all the lost souls in the world,
He came to seek and to save.

06/2013

Jesus And Me

(Chorus)
Strolling along, singing my song,
Thinking about Jesus and me;
The rain may fall; I don't worry at all,
Jesus takes care of me.
The sun may shine, and everything's fine,
I'm happy as I can be;
As I stroll along singing my song,
It's just Jesus and me.
(1)
Jesus purchased my soul a long time ago,
On that cruel old tree;
He made me whole and now I know,
He has set my spirit free.
He forgave my sin and cleansed me within,
The day I called on Him;
Now on Him I wholly depend,
When things start looking dim.
(2)
There are trials I know, grief and woe,
As I stroll along;
But Jesus is there; my troubles He'll bear,
While I sing my song.
I can laugh and sing and know that everything,
Is set for eternity;
Just singing my song all day long,
It's just Jesus and me.

Jesus Came Looking For Me

(1)
Jesus came looking for me,
I was too blind to see;
He wanted to save my soul.
He called and He called,
Each time I stalled;
But Jesus kept looking for me.
(2)
Jesus knocked on my door,
Like so often before;
But I would turn Him away.
The last time He came,
He called my name;
And I asked Him in to stay.
(3)
I opened the door then,
I invited Him in;
He saved my soul that day.
He forgave all my sin,
And changed me within;
He guided me along life's way.
(4)
Now Jesus is here,
Life's way is so clear;
To reach heaven's bright shore.
If Jesus comes knocking for you,
Here's what you do;
Just reach and open the door.

Judgement

(1)
I dreamed I was standing on Judgement Day,
Before the Master and I heard Him say;
"Your name is not written in the Book of Life,
You wasted your time in sin and strife."
(Omit Chorus)
(2)
But, Lord, oh Lord, my name should be there,
I went to church, spent time in prayer;
I was baptized in the water one day,
I listened to what the preacher did say.
(Chorus)
"You only worked for others to see,
The things you did were not for me;
You believed in your mind but not your heart,
Sinner, from me you must depart."
(3)
Oh Lord, my father was a preacher man,
He preached about Jesus and the salvation plan;
He took me to church every time he could,
I taught Sunday School; I tried to be good.
(4)
I sang in the choir; I visited the poor,
Lord, I spread your Word from door to door;
My name must be there in your book,
Please, Lord, please Lord, take one more look.
(5)
I gave my money to charity.

Judgement

"But you never gave your heart to me.
You worked in vain; now it's too late."
Oh Lord, I'll never see heaven's gate.

Knocking At The Door

(1)
"My name is Jesus, I stand at your door and knock.
I try to turn the knob, but I find the door is locked;
If you'll unlock the door and let me come in,
I'll give you life eternal and forgive you all your sin."
(Chorus)
I hear you knockin', but you can't come in,
Why don't you go back where you've always been;
I don't want you here shaking up my home,
Go back down that road and leave me alone.
(2)
My name is Death, and I'm knockin' on your door,
I've come to take you with me; you'll need this house no more;
Jesus came to see you; you turned Him away,
Now Satan's waiting for you; you'll meet him today.
(3)
I hear Jesus knocking'; I'm gonna let Him in,
I want Him to change me from what I've always been;
Give me that life eternal and live within my heart,
Cause I want to have that feelin' that we'll never be apart.
(4)
If Jesus comes a knockin', you better let Him in,
He's come to say, "I love you," and forgive all your sin;
Death will soon come knockin' to take you to your fate,
So open the door for Jesus before it's too late.

10/08/2002

Life's Choices

(Chorus)
If I only knew that tomorrow might be,
The last day I spend on this earth;
Would I be willing to be all I can be,
And live my life for all that it's worth?
(1)
We get so busy in making a life,
We soon forget how to live;
We get caught up in getting all we can,
That we soon forget how to give.
(2)
Life may seem long, but in God's time,
It's only a brief span;
But where we go in eternity,
We make a choice in life while we can.
(3)
You can trust Jesus as your Savior,
He will lead you to heaven's shore;
Or you can go through life and do nothing,
And be lost forevermore.

03/15/2000

Lift Him Up

(1)
Jesus spoke to Nicodemus,
"Ye must be born again."
Living in God's Kingdom,
Turning from your worldly sin.
Letting Christ, your Lord and Master,
Control your heart and mind.
Lift Him up, make Him thine,
Lift Him up all the time;
Lift Him up, lift Him up,
Trusting in His love divine.
(2)
As Moses lifted the brazen serpent,
Before the people one day;
It seems that even now I can hear the Master say,
"Christ must also be lifted,
Before salvation you can find."
Lift Him up, make Him thine,
Lift Him up all the time;
Lift Him up, lift Him up,
Trusting in His love divine.
(3)
God gave us a Redeemer,
He was God's begotten Son;
He fought the devil's battle,
And the victory He won.
The reason this all came to pass,
Was God so loved all mankind;

Lift Him Up

Lift Him up, make Him thine,
Lift Him up all the time;
Lift Him up, lift Him up,
Trusting in His love divine.

Make Me A Temple

(1)
Lord, let my life be an example,
That the world might surely see;
That my body is a Holy Temple,
With my Jesus living in me.
(Chorus)
Make me a temple, dear Jesus,
That my friends may all look and say;
There's a child of God among us,
Who walks with Jesus each day.
(2)
Our bodies are temples they tell me,
God's Spirit lives there, I'm told;
If we have been saved and set free,
So, Lord, cleanse me and make me whole.
(3)
Dear Jesus, make me a temple,
Purge me without and within;
I want to be a living example,
Of what life can be without sin.

06/27/2003

Mary's Lamb

(Chorus) (Start)
Mary had a little lamb,
A little lamb, a little lamb;
Mary had a little lamb,
Born in Bethlehem.
(1)
Jesus is the little lamb's name,
The night He was born the shepherds came;
They left their sheep out on the plain,
They went to see the one the angels proclaimed.
(2)
The Lamb of God was who they saw,
Just a little baby in a cattle stall;
There in a stall where the cattle would eat,
Where God and man came to meet.
(3)
Mary wondered, but she never knew,
The things this little lamb would someday do;
Little did she know as He lay on the hay,
That He would die for us all someday.

12/2012

New Point Of View

(1)
I once was lost and had no direction,
Earthly pleasures were all I ever knew;
Then one day I met Jesus,
Now I have a whole new point of view.
(Chorus)
I've got a different point of view since I met Jesus,
I see things so differently;
Jesus brought me peace and comfort,
When He came to live with me.
(2)
Jesus put His loving arms around me,
He saved me and gave me life anew;
Now I want to serve Him forever,
For now I have a new point of view.
(3)
I'll sing His songs and praise Him,
And trust Him in all I do;
He changed my life completely,
And gave me a new point of view.

05/27/2013
Based on 2 Corinthians 5:17 (KJV)
Therefore if any man be in Christ, he is a new creature: old things are passed away; behold all things are become new.

Nothing's Wrong With Me

(A Ditty)

I aimed at the moon, and I hit the sun,
I just can't seem to get anything done.
What the matter with me?
What's the matter with me?

I went down to the track, and I entered the race,
Slipped and fell flat on my face.
What's the matter with me?
What's the matter with me?

Going down the road fast as I can,
Ran off the pavement; stuck in the van.
What's the matter with me?
What's the matter with me?

Went huntin' for a deer; found a bear,
Ran right off and left him there.
What's the matter with me?
What's the matter with me?

Went to a church, sat on a pew,
Hoping the preacher would soon get through.
What's the matter with me?
What's the matter with me?

Down at the altar on my knees in prayer,

I met my Jesus while I was there.
Nothin's the matter with me.
Nothing's wrong with me.

Now I Live For Jesus

(1)
Now I was a lost sinner when Jesus came along,
He changed my thinking to the right from the wrong;
Now I live for Jesus all the day long.
(Chorus)
Jesus touched me and He saved my soul,
Yes, He touched me and He made me whole;
Now I live for Jesus; I want the world to know.
(2)
Jesus is my Master; oh yes, He's my Lord,
I learned all about Him from His Holy Word;
Now I live for Jesus in such a sweet accord.
(3)
I was unworthy, yet He loved me so,
He died for me many years ago;
Now I'm going to heaven, and I'm ready to go.

09/1998

Oh, What A Savior

(1)
Jesus is so wonderful; He's so wonderful to me,
Yes I truly love Him because He set me free;
Jesus is my Master, my Lord, my King, my Friend,
He gave me life eternal and joy that will never end.
(Chorus)
Oh, what a Savior; oh, what majesty,
Oh, what a great love that He bestowed on me;
Oh, what great mercy; oh, what love divine,
He cared enough about me to save this soul of mine.
(2)
I will always serve Him as a servant serves his King,
I'll bow my knees before Him, and His praises forever sing;
Glory to my Savior, the One who died for all,
You can share His love and mercy if on Him you will call.
(3)
The cross could not defeat Him; He won the victory,
He prayed for our forgiveness as He died on Calvary;
That tomb is now empty; He is no longer there,
We will see Him in His glory at that meeting in the air.

06/2002

On Eagles Wings

(1)
On the wings of eagles as they soar above,
God brings to us His wonderful love;
On the mountain top the eagle builds her nest,
It's a place to go when she needs to rest.
(Chorus)
On eagles' wings born to lofty heights,
To the mountain peak pointing to the sky;
God lifted me up above all my sin,
When I opened the door and bid Him come in.
(2)
Jesus is our resting place,
In Him we can feel His mercy and grace;
Jesus says in Him we can find our rest,
Just like the eagle on the mountain crest.
(3)
Jesus offers His love to you and me,
And just like the eagle, in Him we are free;
His wings of grace are spread so wide,
A multitude of sins His love will hide.
(4)
On eagles' wings born to lofty heights,
To the mountain peak pointing to the sky;
God will lift you up above all your sin,
If you will open your heart and let Him come in.

11/15/2000

Our Savior Lives

(1)
The tomb was empty; Christ was not there,
In her amazement, Mary looked everywhere;
The grave clothes were lying on the death bed,
The napkin was there where they laid His head.
(Chorus)
Glory to God, as we think on these things,
And praise Him forever in the songs that we sing;
Yes, He has ascended to His heavenly home,
Where He rules and reigns from His great white throne.
(2)
Mary started to weep as she turned away,
Then she saw Jesus and she heard Him say;
"Mary, dear Mary, listen to me,
Tell my disciples I'll see them in Galilee."
(3)
Jesus met His disciples in the upper room,
And said to them, "I'll be leaving here soon.
But when I go, I won't leave you alone.
The Comforter will come, you'll not be on your own."
(4)
Oh, when we hear the trumpet blast,
We'll know Jesus is coming back at last;
He'll take all His saints to their heavenly home,
The sinners will be left here all alone.

5/2002

Rocking Alone In An Old Rocking Chair (2 Verses)

(1)
Rocking alone in an old rocking chair,
I see an old mother with silvery hair;
She seemed so neglected by those who should care,
As she rocks all alone in an old rocking chair.

(2)
Her hands are calloused, wrinkled, and old,
A life of hard work is the story that's told;
And I think of angels as I see her there,
Just rocking alone in that old rocking chair.

(3)
Bless her old heart; do you think she'd complain,
Though life has been bitter, she'd live it again;
And always be willing to bear more than her share,
She's just rocking alone in that old rocking chair.

(4)
Now I know some kids in an orphan's home,
Who would think they owned heaven if she was their own;
They'd never be willing to let her sit there,
And rock all alone in that old rocking chair.

The above four verses I never wrote. It's an old song I have known all my life. I do not know the author. These next two verses are mine. I added them to this song because it's the way it was with Mom.

(5)
Reminds me of Mama; she meant the world to me,

I still think of her as she used to be;
In memory I can still see her there,
Rocking alone in her old rocking chair.
(6)
Now she's gone to be with Jesus, I know,
While I'm still waiting for my time to go;
I know she'll be waiting for me up there,
While she patiently rocks in her new rocking chair.
(Tag)
Yes, Mama's now rocking in her new rocking chair.

Sing About Jesus

(Chorus)
We sing about the red-nosed reindeer,
We sing about jingle bells;
We sing about old Santa Clause,
Not the story that we need to tell.
Is a newborn babe in a manger,
There in old Bethlehem;
We'll sing praises to this little one,
We'll sing glory to His name.
(1)
The angels did not appear to the rich man,
Nor did they go to the palace of the King;
They came to the lowly shepherds,
Out on the desert plain.
Glory to God in the highest,
Peace on earth; good will to all;
They found baby Jesus in Bethlehem,
Lying in a cattle stall.
(2)
The shepherds came very quickly,
On their knees they did bow;
And worshipped this newborn baby,
They never asked who or how.
He came two thousand years ago,
To be our Savior and King;
So when we think about Christmas,
It's to Him we all should sing.

Sinner, Please Don't Wait

(1)
I got saved this morning,
When I went to Sunday church;
Now I feel so good all over,
There's nothing about me that hurts.
The preacher preached about heaven,
Then he preached about hell;
Well, the message was so clear and plain,
I remember every word so well.
(Chorus)
I'm gonna find me a river,
I'm gonna be baptized;
Yes, I'm gonna be different,
When out of that water I rise.
I'm gonna tell everybody about Jesus,
I'm gonna serve Him the best I can;
Then folks can look at me and say,
"There goes a God-loving man."
(2)
I want people to know about Jesus,
And about His amazing grace;
I want them to know on Calvary,
He died just to take our place.
So give your heart to Jesus,
Before it's too late;
Death is just around the corner,
O, sinner, please don't wait.

Take Jesus

(1)
When the storm clouds gather all about you,
And the waves, they toss you to and fro;
Open your heart and turn to Jesus,
For He is the best friend you can know.
(Chorus)
Take Jesus as your guiding light,
He will lead and direct you through the night;
Over the rough seas and through the stormy sky,
Jesus will lead you to heaven on high.
(2)
When your friends turn you down and you feel so alone;
Won't you then take Jesus as your very own?
But when everything seems to be happy and bright,
Don't forget it was Jesus who made it all right.
(3)
In heaven there will be no night,
No sorrow, no sadness, no sickness, nor fright;
If you will take Jesus by the hand,
Someday He will lead you to that wonderful land.

The Bird In The Window

(Chorus)
There's a bird in the window, seeing all you do,
That bird in the window is gonna tell on you;
So live your life for Jesus every moment of the day,
Then that bird in the window has nothing bad to say.
(1)
Be kind to your neighbor, lend a helping hand,
Let them all know on God's Word you stand;
Be honest in your dealings; always be fair,
That bird in the window will tell it everywhere.
(2)
If cheatin' and lying seems to be your lifestyle,
The world will know about it in just a little while;
That bird in the window will have so much to share,
So give your heart to Jesus and trust His loving care.
(3)
If that bird in the window fails to see all you do,
Remember God in heaven has His eyes on you;
He knows your every action; He hears every word,
You have never made a sound that He hasn't heard.
(4)
What that bird has to say may not to much amount,
But God keeps a record; it's the one that will count;
So keep these things in mind as you go along life's way,
Be careful what you do and watch what you say.

Ecclesiastes 10:20

The Bird In The Window

Curse not the King, no not in thy thought; and curse not the rich in thy bedchamber; for a bird of the air shall carry the voice, and that which hath wings shall tell the matter (KJV)

5/2005

The Brighter Side

(Chorus)
Stay on the brighter side,
Keep on the brighter side,
As you travel down the road of life.
It will help you day by day,
If you will take time to pray,
And stay on the brighter side.
(1)
The world is darkness all about,
Full of worry, full of doubt,
But Jesus is always very near.
He can make you free and make you shout,
And turn your life inside out,
Yes, Jesus can take away your fear.
(2)
Jesus brightens our road,
Leads the way and takes our load,
Yes, we must stay on the brighter side.
The seeds of faith must be spread,
As we shine our light ahead,
And we stay on the brighter side.

03/06/2004

The Change

(1)
He turned my frown into a smile,
He made my whole life worthwhile,
Jesus has done so much for me.
He changed my wants and desire,
And gave me a new life entire,
Now the whole world can see.

(2)
He changed the direction I was going,
As I wandered about, not even knowing,
That I was lost for eternity.
Jesus took the worry from my brow,
Then He took time to show me how
To live forever and be free.

(3)
My goals in life have been changed,
A new home in Glory has been arranged,
When I asked Jesus to save my soul.
My sins have all been forgiven,
My new life is now worth livin',
Jesus took all the pieces and made me whole.

(4)
Sin and evil possessed my mind,
Lust and cravings most all the time,
But Jesus took these things away from me.
He made me into a brand new creature,
Then He called me to be a preacher,
Now that's all I ever want to do.

(Tag)
He turned my frown into a smile,
He made my whole life worthwhile,
Jesus has done so much for me.

11/09/2005

The Devil Ain't A Gonna Bother Me

(GOING DOWN THE ROAD)

(Chorus)
I'm going down the road feeling good, good, good.
I'm going down the road feeling good.
I'm going down the road feeling good, good, good,
And the devil ain't a gonna bother me.
(1)
The road goes to heaven on high, high, high.
The road goes to heaven up in the sky.
I'm going to heaven when I die, die, die,
And the devil ain't a gonna stop me.
(2)
Jesus died and saved my soul, soul, soul.
Jesus died and saved me and made me whole.
Jesus got a place for me with streets of gold, gold, gold.
And the devil ain't a gonna get to me.
(3)
I've got a place in glory I know, know, know,
In the Holy Bible, Jesus tells me so.
Now when He calls me, I'll go, go, go,
And the devil ain't a gonna stop me.

07/01/2003

The Dream

(1)
I was standing here before the Master,
With head bowed staring at my feet;
Then I heard the voice of my Master,
Saying, "What hast thou done for me."
With trembling voice then I answered,
"Lord, I have gone astray.
I have followed in the devil's footsteps;
All my sins at thy feet I lay."
(Chorus)
Yes, Jesus is the Master; He is God's begotten Son,
On the cross of Calvary He died, yet the victory He won;
For now He has arisen from that borrowed grave,
And I will always serve Him for my lost soul He has saved.
(2)
Then the Master reached and touched me,
He placed His hand upon my head;
"Go forth, my son, now and serve me,
And I will lead you instead."
I awoke and found I had been sleeping,
But His presence I could still feel;
Then I realized I had been dreaming,
A dream that seemed so very real.
(3)
Now I seek to serve Him,
Going where He says go;
Doing the things that He tells me,
For I love my Master so.

The Dream

When He comes in His glory,
I will be ready to meet Him;
I shall see Him there before me,
As I leave this world of sin.

(4)
Listen while I tell you brothers,
Sisters, too, won't you believe;
How this dream now has changed me,
And opened my eyes that I could see.
Oh, I wish that you would serve Him,
And for you I will pray;
That you will reach out and touch Him,
And let Him lead you every day.

(About 1965)

The Good Shepherd

(Chorus)
I'm just a sheep in the pasture of Jesus,
When the wolf shall howl and the lion shall roar;
I'll be safe in the arms of Jesus,
He will watch over me forevermore.
(1)
I am His sheep; He is my shepherd,
He's always there; it's written in His word;
He takes care of me wherever I go,
He is the Good Shepherd; I love Him so.
(2)
The sheep know the Shepherd, and He knows them,
I became His lamb when I trusted Him;
He knows my voice when He hears me talk,
He keeps me from falling wherever I walk.
(3)
Is He your shepherd, are you His sheep?
In His pasture the water flows clear and deep;
The heavens are bright; the grass grows green,
In His presence the air is fresh and clean.
(4)
Someday He's coming to gather His flock,
Whose faith has endured like a solid rock;
To live in that pasture on heaven's bright shore,
And praise our good Shepherd forevermore.

02/26/2000

The Sky Is The Limit

(Chorus)
The sky is the limit on how high you can go,
Put your trust in Jesus and then you can know;
That heaven is there waiting for me and for you,
I'm ready to go; are you ready too?
(1)
There is no limit to the sky above,
And there is no end to God's mercy and love;
The sky is the limit to what God has in store,
For all His children when we reach heaven's shore.
(2)
Jesus ascended into the blue sky
And went on to His Father in heaven on high;
Someday He'll be coming back again,
He'll span the great sky to gather all His saints in.

05/30/2009

Walk With Me, Jesus

(1)
Life gets so dreary as I struggle along,
Sometimes I get the feeling that I just can't go on;
But I know you're with me; I'm never alone,
Walk with me, Jesus, until you call me home.
(Chorus)
Remove the mountains of troubles I face,
Let me feel your presence here in this place;
Hear me please, Jesus, as I bow to pray,
Walk with me, Jesus, every step of the way.
(2)
Seems that cheatin' and lying is on every hand,
Stealing and killing is so common to man;
Wars and turmoil that I don't understand,
Walk with me, Jesus, through this wicked land.
(3)
Someday He'll be coming; peace and joy will abound,
Singing and praising Jesus; what a wonderful sound;
No pain and no sorrow; no tears will be found,
Walk with me, Jesus, don't let me fall down.

02/10/2004

Walking On High Ground

(1)
I was once a drunkard; my life I lived in vain,
I felt such deep depression; I suffered mental pain;
I thought no one loved me; there was no one to care,
But thanks to my Jesus, He was standing there.
(Chorus)
Now I'm walking, walking, walking, walking on high ground,
Feeling more happiness than ever I had found;
Life is so much brighter each and every day,
As I travel through this world with Jesus leading all the way.
(2)
I was in such bad shape, I wanted to die,
Satan thought he had me, but Jesus heard my cry;
I was tattered and battered and in a deep dark pit,
Then Jesus came along and took me out of it.
(3)
It will always amaze me, the things my God can do,
How He could take my life so worthless and make it all anew;
He took me from Satan's dungeon of sorrow and sin,
And changed me completely without and within.

11/02/1999

Walking On The Water Of The River Of Life

(Chorus)
Walking on the water of the river of life,
Winds are a blowing troubles and strife;
But I'll just keep going 'till I reach the other side,
Walking on the water of the river of life.
(1)
Jesus walked on the water on the Sea of Galilee,
Peter walked there too as long as Jesus he could see;
He took his eyes off Jesus, but the Lord heard his cry,
He started sinking, but the Lord was by his side.
(2)
Once I was a sinner, wandering to and fro,
Not ever knowing which way to go;
Then I saw Jesus; now I'm satisfied,
Walking on the water of the river of life.
(3)
Walking on the water of the river of life,
Trouble all around me, I hold my head up high;
Looking to Jesus, thinking about the other side,
Walking on the water of the river of life.

09/08/2011

What People See

(1)
I want to be different on life's trail,
Having Jesus with me, I shall not fail;
In this sinful world, I want others to know,
Jesus is with me wherever I go.

(2)
Some people go to church; they pray and sing.
They talk about Jesus and praise His name;
But with worldly friends they fit so well,
If they know Jesus, it's hard to tell.

(Chorus)
Does everybody know I'm a Christian?
Does everybody know who I stand for?
Does everybody see Jesus in me?
I want to be like Him more and more.

(3)
If you're ashamed of Him, He's ashamed of you,
He knows your thoughts, what you say and do;
He knows if you're His and if you're true,
Trust in Jesus now; He's watching you.

04/11/2007

When God Calls My Name

(Chorus)
When God looks down and calls my name,
And the angels all begin to sing;
I know I'll be going home at last,
This earthly life will all be past.
(1)
As I kneel before the throne of grace,
I'll see my master face to face;
I'll want to hear Him say, "A job well done.
Welcome home, my faithful son."
(2)
I'll hear His voice loud and plain,
When God looks down and calls my name;
After all these years, there's one thing I know,
When God calls me, I'll be ready to go.
(3)
I've seen the depths of the ocean's floor,
I've seen the stars in the sky;
But when the Master opens heaven's door,
What a sight will greet my eyes.

06/01/2008

When It's Gospel Singing Time In Heaven

(1)
When it's gospel singing time in heaven,
What a glorious time awaits for me;
I'll stand and sing my songs for Jesus,
While the angels add their harmony.
(Chorus)
While David plays his harp there for us,
Gabriel's trumpet joins the melody;
The angels singing around the throne of Jesus,
Oh, what a gospel singing time that will be.
(2)
We won't need a special invitation,
Nor a schedule will we need to see;
When God calls us all to heaven,
We will know when the singing will be.
(3)
With the cymbals, the horns, and tambourines,
Oh, what a beautiful sound;
I can hear the band now it seems,
It's gospel singing time all around.

08/05/2003

When The Rooster Crowed

(1)
The disciples were with Jesus in Gethsemane,
They lay there and slept while Jesus was in agony;
Jesus was bearing such a heavy load,
Yet Peter denied Him before the rooster crowed.
(Chorus)
When the rooster crowed, Peter saw what he had done,
He had turned his back on God's only Son;
He saw the beating and the blood as it flowed,
It all came to Peter when the rooster crowed.
(2)
They took Jesus up on Mount Calvary,
As He hung on the cross, He prayed for you and for me;
The people all there soon would know,
What Peter felt when the rooster crowed.
(3)
You can drift through life thinking all is well,
But when the going gets rough, it's then you can tell;
You may have followed Jesus on the dusty road,
But will you deny Him before the rooster crows?

03/23/2002

When The Wind Blows

(1)
My faith is much like the blowing wind,
You may not see it, but you can see where it's been;
It has brought me through many storms in my life,
Thru' sickness and death, struggles and strife.
(Chorus)
When the wind blows, you see the falling leaves,
You can feel the coolness of the blowing breeze;
The Holy Spirit is like the wind as it blows,
Where it will take you, only God knows.
(2)
Jesus asked the disciples, "Where is your faith?"
When the storm was raging and they were afraid;
The wind was blowing; the waves were so high,
But Jesus was there, and He heard their cry.
(3)
If you want to make it through storms of all kind,
Have Jesus in your heart and faith on your mind;
God works in ways that nobody knows,
But keep faith in Him when the wind blows.

04/06/2009

Where The Milk And Honey Flows

(1)
Just over there across the river Jordan,
It's the land of promise I have heard;
Where the milk and honey there is flowing,
According to God's Holy Word.
(Chorus)
I want to go over the river Jordan,
There's milk and honey there I know;
And I'm getting oh so hungry,
I want to be where the milk and honey flow.
(2)
When God calls me to come on over,
I'm hungry now and ready to go;
Then I will cross over the river Jordan,
Where the milk and the honey flow.
(3)
When I get there, God will feed me,
With the milk and honey and grapes that grow;
There will be enough to satisfy my hunger,
There where the milk and honey flow.
(4)
When I sit down at God's table,
Surrounded by that heavenly glow;
I shall dine there with Jesus, my Savior,
Where the milk and the honey flows.

10/04/2000

Will You Readily Grasp Him By The Hand

(1)
Jesus shed His life's blood for you and me,
When He died on the cross of Calvary;
When they pierced Him in the side,
He was pleading as He died,
For us to readily grasp Him by the hand.
(Chorus)
Will you readily grasp Him by the hand,
When He reaches down from that promised land?
When He reaches down from above,
And offers you His love,
Will you readily grasp Him by the hand?
(2)
Now He has gone to His Father up on high,
But the Bible still tells of His cry;
For us to turn from wrong to right,
And believe in His might.
Will you readily grasp Him by the hand?
(3)
He tells us in His Word He'll come again,
To take us from this world of sin;
Though we know not the hour,
We must surely trust His power,
And readily grasp Him by the hand.

Between Your Heart And Mine

(1)
Between your heart and mine,
There's a river of love flowing;
It will last through all time,
As it keeps growing and growing.
It lightens our face; it sparkles in our eyes.
Love found its place in the center of our lives.
(Chorus)
A love that's so good and sure,
A love that's sweet; a love that's pure;
I never knew a love could be so fine,
As the love that's flowing between your heart and mine.
(2)
As I hold your hand and look into your eyes,
I see and understand, and I realize;
That though my love for you is true,
Your love belongs to me too.
Our love for each other is wonderful and fine,
As it keeps on flowing between your heart and mine.
(3)
Between your heart and mine is a chain that's strong,
It will bind us forever; we will never go wrong;
I wake up each morning with a glow on my face,
Thinking this world is a beautiful place.
I see the beautiful flowers and hear the singing birds chime,
All because of this love between your heart and mine.

Fonder, More Fonder

(1)
My heart grows fonder, more fonder,
For you, dear, yes, for you, dear;
Your lips grow sweeter, more sweeter,
For you, dear, yes, for you, dear.
(2)
I think I love you, but sometimes I wonder,
But for you, fear, my heart grows fonder;
Your lips grow sweeter, more sweeter,
For me, dear, oh yes, for me, dear.
(3)
When you're not with me, how I miss you.
I want to kiss you, I really want you;
My heart grows fonder, more fonder,
For you, dear, oh yes, for you, dear.
(4)
Your lips grow sweeter, more sweeter,
For me, dear, oh yes, for me, dear;
I think you love me; don't ask me why,
Maybe it's that sparkle that's in your eye.

Headaches And Heartaches

(Chorus)
Headaches and heartaches is all that I get from you.
Headaches when you're with me,
And heartaches when you're with someone new.
I gave you fine things and tried to love you too.
(1)
You tell me you love me, but I know it's not true.
My head still hurts and my heart feels so blue.
You're always leaving me suffering in this misery,
And headaches and heartaches is all that you give to me.
(2)
I gave you my promises and all of my vows,
But none of them mean anything to you now.
My heart is aching and full of agony,
'Cause headaches and heartaches are all that you give to me.
(3)
Aspirins may help this pain in my head,
But the heartaches will last until I am dead.
I know that you don't care which way it will be,
'Cause headaches and heartaches are all that you give to me.
(4)
Tonight when you leave me here at home,
Don't think that I will be all alone.
I've found a new friend who loves and cares for me,
She'll be over to give me her company.
(5)
You'll find the house locked and a note on the door,
Saying, "This is not your home anymore.

Headaches And Heartaches

Go find your lovers wherever they may be,
'Cause headaches and heartaches is all you gave to me."

(1949)

I Just Can't Get Away From You

(1)
I love you, my darling, and I always will,
My heart within me just won't be still;
My mind wants to wander; my heart just won't go,
I'll never want another, I want you to know.
(Chorus)
Love is too strong, passions too high,
We've been together too long; can't say goodbye;
Together in life we'll make it through,
I just can't get away from you.
(2)
Sometimes I think that you don't care,
But my heart would sink if you weren't there;
I can't go away, no matter what you do,
I'll have to stay and hope you love me too.
(3)
Let us pretend that we just met,
Let troubles all end and bad times forget;
I'll be yours and you'll be mine,
All through the years 'till the end of time.

I'm In Love With You

(1)
Oh, I have never met anyone in this whole wide world who could compare with you,
There are plenty pretty girls in this world, but none of them will do;
If you ever need somebody, dear, I wish you'd call on me,
It would make me feel so wanted, dear, and as happy as can be.

(2)
I've loved you since the day we met, I want it understood,
And I would even marry you yet if I only could;
They say a married man is happy, dear, if he has a loving wife,
But I guess I'll always feel so drear the rest of my natural life.

(3)
It's not because of your pretty little face or the cute little things you do,
But in your heart I want a place because I'm in love with you;
We used to go out for a ride every Sunday afternoon,
Now all our fun as died; it all ended too soon.

(4)
I want you more and more each day as time travels on,
I don't see how I can go on this way; I want you for my own;
If you don't hurry and wed me soon, I know I'll probably die,
I want to be your happy groom; won't you give me your reply?

No Money

(Chorus)
If you're lookin' for money, honey,
I've got none it's plain to see;
So if you're lookin' for money, honey,
Don't be lookin' at me.
(1)
Let me tell you something, honey,
Money is hard to get;
So if you're lookin' for money, honey,
I don't have any yet.
(2)
I work hard for a little pay,
To buy a thing or two;
So if you're lookin' for money, honey
I've got none here for you.
(3)
I'm on the job every day,
Working my fingers to the bone;
So if you're lookin' for money, honey,
You'll have to get it own your own.
(4)
There's never enough to go around,
With all the bills I have to pay;
So if you're lookin' for money, honey,
There's nothing more to say.

Nothing To Do - (After Surgery)

My wife's gone every day; she's working away,
Trying to make a dollar or two;
While I sit here alone, in our humble home,
With nothing to do.

I've got nothing to do and all day to do it,
But I just can't seem to get around to it.

It's not that I'm lazy; I never have been,
I've worked hard and long on days without end;
But since I've had surgery and trying to recoup,
Sitting around with nothing to do.

I've got nothing to do and all day to do it,
But I just can't seem to get around to it.

Oh, I see things around me that need to be done,
Some things of work and some of fun;
But friends, let me leave you with a word or two,
It just ain't no fun with nothing to do.

I've got nothing to do and all day to do it,
But I just can't seem to get around to it.

09/24/2013

The Blue Valley Waltz

(1)
The song that they sang when I gave you the ring,
Was the beautiful blue valley waltz;
The music was so gay as we swirled and we swayed,
To the beautiful blue valley waltz.
(Chorus)
The tune I'll never forget,
I often sing it yet,
'Tis the beautiful blue valley waltz.
(2)
Beneath the stars up above,
We spoke of our love,
While they were playing the blue valley waltz.
You promised to be my bride,
While we were dancing side by side,
To the beautiful blue valley waltz.
(3)
I've been happy all the time,
Since you promised to be mine,
While they were playing the blue valley waltz.
It keeps coming back to me,
Just as plain as can be,
The beautiful blue valley waltz.